Affordable

Thinking critically and differently
about affordable housing

Tayo Odunsi

KINETIC

Copyright © 2018 by Tayo Odunsi
All rights reserved. This book or any portion thereof
may not be reproduced or used in any manner whatsoever
without the express written permission of the publisher
except for the use of brief quotations in a book review.

Authors Photograph: Seun O
Book Layout: Olaniyi Timilehin
Front Cover Design: Tunji Agboola and Olaniyi Timilehin

Printed in Nigeria
First Printing, 2018

ISBN 978-1-78808-264-8

KINETIC

Kinetic Books
29 Mambilla Street, Maitama, Abuja. Nigeria.

affordable@kinetic.com.ng
www.kinetic.com.ng

//REVIEWS

This book gives 41 thought-provoking pointers that everyone involved in housing should read, and isn't that all of us? As the book shows, housing is all about Government, Private Sector, Professionals, the Community and the Individual – when it comes to housing each one of us fits at least one of these roles. Housing affects us all.

The book combines an insight of some theory but its particular strength is that it refers to the practice in order to get you thinking beyond what do all these concepts really mean to the reality of affordable housing

Ellen Geurts – Lecturer, Institute of Housing and Urban Development Studies, Erasmus University, The Netherlands

In beautiful prose, Affordable paints a vivid picture of the five essential elements of affordable housing, which must work together in a balanced harmony if we are to put a lasting dent in the current dearth we face. The author does a fine job of explaining the distinct yet cross cutting roles of each player in what could yet be a beautiful dance. Policy makers, students of the trade, investors and even speculators would do well to invest time in reading this scholarly work.

Kola Aina – Founder, Ventures Platform

Affordable is an eminently readable treatise on how the Nigerian housing crisis (it is a crisis), can be tackled. Tayo Odunsi skilfully uses anecdotes to keep the reader interested but is methodical and scholarly in identifying the essential parties and their roles in affordable housing. Prepare to have your settled notions on housing challenged.

Dipo Davies – Publisher, Castles Weekly Magazine

Affordable is a book that could be described as a 'new normal' in the housing lexicon in Nigeria. It is a passionate and painstaking effort by Tayo Odunsi at deconstructing the nebulous concept called affordable housing, offering fresh insights into pathways to housing delivery.

The simplicity of its language rendered in fluid, lucid and expository expressions easily gives the book away as a guide or compass to discovering what its possible in developing countries, when and where there is direction, duty, activity, professionalism and commitment as captured in its 'pentagon' theory.

Essentially, this is a pointer to all of us that to make affordable housing happen, the house buyer must be as involved as the supplier, financier, enabler and regulator such that if houses are not affordable as they are today, it is because one line in the 'pentagon' is either missing or dysfunctional.

Chuka Uroko – Property Editor, BusinessDay

This is an excellent book and very timely for developing countries as it provides practical solutions to the affordable housing conundrum. It is very well researched and easy to read and clearly talks to the issues"

Dennis Papa Odenyi Quansah – Consultant, EDGE Africa Implementation, International Finance Corporation

This book brings theoretically sound, realistic and thought-provoking perspectives to the discourse on affordable housing in short and well framed chapters. This unique approach of the book to a crucial matter like housing is in itself a triumph.

What Tayo Odunsi offers through Affordable are perspectives that clarify the mutually exclusive roles of key stakeholders in the housing space which should help both our comprehension and implementation of these roles for the common good. With these thoughts in practice, the transformation of our housing sector seems imminent. This is by far the easiest yet thought provoking book you will ever read on affordable housing.

Dr. Adeyinka Adewale – Lecturer, Henley Business School, University of reading, UK

Tayo succinctly captures the role of the critical stakeholders in the process to deliver affordable housing by looking back at what has worked in different countries. This book provides much food for thought for anyone searching for ideas on how to make it work today.

Wole Famurewa - Fellow, Strategic Communications & Stakeholder Engagement, Nigerian Economic Summit Group.

This is more than a book on affordable housing. Affordable is a well crafted and very informative read for early starters, a masterclass for professionals, and a handbook for the government and the private sector. One thing is for sure, Tayo Odunsi makes sure there is something for everyone in here, to help make better decisions that will contribute to achieving affordable housing in any developing nation.

Bez - Award-winning Music Artist

Since the commencement of my career as a real estate professional, the issue of affordability has stared me in the face. Characteristically, I've jumped in, thought deeply, sought out creative methods but failed to offer a solution that I can dispense to everyone seeking affordable housing.

In 2016 I was led to attend a course at the Institute of Housing and Urban Development, Rotterdam. It was there that it hit me. Affordable housing cannot be solved by one party or even two.

Often times we look to the government or developers to produce affordable housing, but both parties in themselves don't have the secret sauce. Affordable housing has five sides; five distinct but important players that make it emerge and sustainable.

I thank God for opening my eyes to what my teachers at IHS couldn't teach me. I thank him for leading me to them to prepare my eyes and ears to birth "Affordable". I thank IHS for offering me a partial fellowship to attend the DSHP 2016 course. To the course coordinators – Ellen Guerts and Julia Skinner as well as all the other teachers and speakers, thank you for the life changing 3-week immersion.

To the chair of the research board – Prof. Omirin, the leaders (Osagie & Ayo) and team at Northcourt Real Estate; thank you for your support and permission to allow me research and write this book. Thanks to my present and past research analysts – Nathan and Anu, my Editor – Cathy and my close pals Yinka, Tunde, Busola, Timi, Femi, Jide, Dele, Bido, Misan and Kola for all the encouragement and strategy ideas! PG, thank you for being an inspiring big brother and mentor. Thanks to all other friends I may have left out, please forgive me, as your support is deeply appreciated.

Special thanks to my parents and siblings for their special variant of support and double special thanks to my lovely wife – Busayo, without whom I would have quit writing after the first chapter.

// PREFACE

This book delineates the roles of the five essential participants in delivering affordable housing: the Government, the Private Sector, Professionals, the Community, and the Individual. Each chapter describes what the particular participant needs to do, or to view differently, so that sustainable affordable housing can be achieved.

The book is action-oriented, with the various action points set in a format to be acted upon independently by any player, even if some or all of the other essential players are not yet on board.

This book draws on experiences from European, Latin American and African contexts. It's a book designed to help you to think critically about housing issues and to think differently about housing delivery.

// TABLE OF CONTENTS

Conclusion: 143

Notes: 149

// INTRODUCTION

Like a Pentagon

Recalling elementary geometry, a pentagon is a five-sided object typically linked by similar but distinct straight lines. Pentagons can be equilateral or non-equilateral – having the same length of sides or otherwise. Often times, any five-sided object is mistaken for a pentagon, but a five-sided object with one or more curved lines is not a pentagon. Similarly, a five-sided object with one or more disjointed lines is not a pentagon. A pentagon is made of five 'similar but distinct' straight and connected lines – just like an affordable housing system.

There are five essential participants in delivering affordable housing – the Government, the Private Sector, Professionals, the Community and the Individual. This "pentagonal" distinction of affordable housing players is essential because each party, like the lines of a pentagon, are distinct yet linked. They have the direct responsibility for affordable housing to be delivered and to be sustainable.

It is intuitive that each role is inter-related. Governments, the private sector, professionals and the community are all made up of individuals. But at the most basic worldview of a person, he stands alone as an individual, having personal preferences and perspectives that are not necessarily those of his professional, communal or political class. Likewise, professionals and the private sector may be said to be the same. However, a distinction must be made between the members of the built environment professions that have fiduciary responsibility for the emergence of homes and cities, versus the rest of the private sector that are not necessarily inclined to participate in this way.

The government is a community but the community is not the government. The government is made of elected, appointed and hired personnel, who take charge of creating and enforcing state policy. A community, on the other hand, is a social unit largely created by co-location, a single but highly important factor that produces shared interests and perspectives.

All five parties at their various 'offices' have major roles to play if affordable housing is to be sustainable.

Depending on which part of the world you are located in, the government may be an affordable housing initiator, enabler, regulator or even developer. While it's held in the public domain that a Jack-of-all-trades is master of none, governments of most developing or underdeveloped countries are, by far, the wealthiest entities in their nations. This means they may have the resources to take on each role in the housing value chain. Either way, governments play a crucial role in housing development, and even more so in ensuring that it is affordable.

The Professionals are the builders, architects, surveyors and engineers that bring housing and communities into existence. Their expertise and perspectives are required from the starting point to make housing either affordable or not.

Irrespective of who conceptualises an affordable housing project, the Private Sector is required at some stage of the venture to ensure that it the project is built and completed. The private sector consists of developers, financiers, investors and managers of affordable housing developments. They are not necessarily trained professionals in design or construction, but they have the business and social innovativeness to structure and manage a development process in more effective and efficient ways than the public sector.

However, the effectiveness and efficiency of the private sector typically comes at a higher cost and requires the watchful eyes of the public to keep prices affordable, with respect to not only the built houses but also the maintenance and management of the development post-construction. This role is best played by the Community. It is the community members who pay, so they are the best watches. The community's power-in-numbers, if focused, can take on governments, developers and other private sector players much more effectively than any one individual can.

But the Individual must choose. The prerogative of

affordable housing belongs to each single individual: Is housing a right or a privilege? Can housing be affordable or should it be affluent? Do I act or stay passive? For housing to be affordable, the individual must hold a sustainable view of housing and then act out this paradigm.

What each participant needs to do, or needs to view differently, in order for sustainable affordable housing to be achieved, varies quite significantly. Each player may act independently even when some or all of the other essential players are yet to get on board. The magnitude of input also differs across locations and scenarios. Similar but different, direct but linked – like a pentagon – are the five essential participants in delivering sustainable affordable housing.

PART 1
// THE GOVERNMENT

ONE

Housing Initiators, Enablers, Providers or Regulators?

Governments play a major role in providing housing for the people. They initiate housing projects by creating city plans that others follow; they enable housing by providing land resources to private developers; they provide housing directly through public housing development schemes; and they regulate all housing development activities through physical planning enforcement.

But if the Jack-of-all-Trades is the master of none, should government be the housing initiator, enabler, provider, and also the regulator? These roles are all very critical and necessary, but they also entail a large workload, and one requiring significant will and skill. On the other hand, if government, with its enormous resource-base, takes on all these tasks, it can at best be akin to a general practitioner; and yet housing needs specialists handling each and every key aspect of the value chain.

Dutch researchers tell the fine story of how after the introduction of the Housing Act of 1901, the Netherlands Government, through social housing associations and municipal housing associations, moved to provide housing for its citizens. Government's influence on the planning and production process was very hands-on.

By the 1970s, the government reviewed its role in social housing and reasoned it should not be undertaking tasks that could be carried out more efficiently by other organisations. Consequently, the social housing organisations were privatised, thereby decentralising authorisations and responsibilities, and giving them liberty to make their own policies. This was taken a step further in 1995, when in exchange for future subsidies payable to the Housing Associations in the sum of almost 16 billion Euros, the Dutch government offset the outstanding loans owed by the existing social and municipal housing authorities.

These changes created both successes and failures. The chief failure was the financial mismanagement by the leadership of some social housing companies. Consequently, in 2015, the Dutch government again changed its point of view and created a new law aimed at restricting the roles of social housing organisations to social housing only and further clarifying rents chargeable and the supervisory roles of the government.

Drawing from the experience of the Netherlands, key shifts in housing policies and roles of the government are visible – from being primarily housing providers to initiators, and then enablers, and more recently regulators. One key lesson is that it is critical for any government to understand its prevailing limitations and possibilities, as well as those of its available private partners, when it is determining what stage of the social or affordable housing value chain it will retain.

As in any game or sport, the role of the Umpire is the most noble. The referee participates fully but is not a competitor, and so has the ability to ensure equity and fairness for all. This is the one role that should never be abdicated by governments in ensuring housing is delivered affordably.

TWO

A Healthy Housing Delivery System

Sickness and disease illustrate clearly that something is wrong. Disease is a disorder or dysfunction in a part or system of a living thing, including humans. Like the human body, housing delivery is a connected system of different organs and parts. Housing delivery is an interdisciplinary endeavour that requires a myriad of members and groups within a society to be successful. Where one is not functioning properly or at all, the system breaks down.

The Institute of Housing and Urban Development Studies in Rotterdam maintains that there are seven components of a housing delivery system. Each component is different but is irreplaceable and critical to sustainable housing delivery in any location.

Authorizations

Imagine your favourite professional sport played without a referee or umpire; it would most likely transit from recreation to war. Legal authorities play a critical role in ensuring urban development is planned, equitable and pleasing. They ensure new developments adhere to zoning laws, health and safety legislations, and other land use considerations. They also regulate who has access to land and they enforce that access.

Land

Land is not just a physical resource; it confers a legal right that can be exchanged, in part, for a period of time or as security to obtain capital. Land acquisition is the first step to housing provision, hence making it a key component of the housing delivery system. According to the Peruvian economist Hernando De Soto, the potency of secure land ownership to attract capital is the key driver that enables first world countries to garner capital.

Infrastructure

Homes need much more than walls, floors, doors, windows and a roof in order to make them habitable. They also need much more other than internal features like interior design and furniture. For a house to be a home, it needs infrastructure: accessibility via roads, connection to power and water, drainage and a sewage system. Where these are available, housing delivery is less hectic and less expensive. Where they do not exist, the result is a broken housing system.

Public Facilities

In addition to infrastructure, the suitability and quality

of houses in any location is primarily determined by the availability and quality of its public facilities. The presence of educational, healthcare, recreational, shopping and other public amenities helps make a house a place for living.

Labour Force
Houses don't build themselves, at least not yet. They are built by a blend of intellectual and manual labour. Intellectual labour providers such as Architects, Engineers and Surveyors are integral to the proper and sustainable construction of homes. Equally important are the manual labour providers, such as masons, carpenters, bar-benders and labourers, who execute the design or instructions of the intellectual workers.

Building Materials
The availability of good building materials at an affordable price and in sufficient quantity can sometimes be a challenge. Often times, certain locations are restricted in the type of building materials that can be used due to technology or climate limitations. This is where the local manufacturing sector must team up with the built environment sector to ensure the best and most affordable materials are made available for sustainable construction. Often times, these two sectors don't speak to each other, and the result is usually malignant for the housing delivery system.

Financing
Money pays for most, if not all, of the housing delivery components. The way money is sourced is called financing and this may be broadly classified to either debt or equity. Debt is essentially a loan, which is repaid in full with interest.

Equity on the other hand is an investment, which is repaid with profit if the transaction is profitable; otherwise the parties share the loss in proportion to their initial investment or agreed terms. Financing is required to purchase land, construct homes, or buy a home that is already constructed. The presence and buoyancy of a housing finance system in a country has a significant effect on the buoyancy of the housing delivery system in that country. In fact, show me a country with a buoyant and well-structured housing finance system and I'll show you a country with a buoyant and well-structured housing delivery system.

As human eyes differ from human legs, so each housing component stands alone and is even sometimes categorised as a different sector of the economy, yet each component plays an integral role in the concert of housing delivery.

THREE

Dynamic Housing Policies

"I am not an advocate for frequent changes in laws and Constitutions. But laws and institutions must go hand in hand with the progress of the human mind. As that becomes more developed, more enlightened, as new discoveries are made, new truths discovered and manners and opinions change, with the change of circumstances, institutions must advance also to keep pace with the times. We might as well require a man to wear still the coat which fitted him when a boy as civilized society to remain ever under the regimen of their barbarous ancestors."

The above quote is an excerpt from a letter written by Thomas Jefferson, one of the founding fathers of the United States of America, the first secretary of state, and subsequently the third president. Thomas Jefferson was an astute policy maker and writer, credited as the principal author of the Declaration of Independence – the very policy document that birthed the United States.

When a man such as President Jefferson, who at the time of his death had authored cardinal federal and state policies, states categorically that laws and institutions need to progress in line with the times, he should be taken very seriously.

Also to be taken very seriously is the Dutch housing system. The Netherlands has one of the most organised and structured housing sectors in the world. Sixty percent of Dutch residents are owner-occupiers; 7% rent; and 33% live in rented social housing – according to the State of Housing in the EU 2015 report. The same report shows that the Netherlands has the highest number of social housing properties in Europe with about 2.4 million social housing units, the second highest being Austria with 800,000 – which is a whopping 67% lower.

But the Netherlands didn't achieve this feat by luck. For one, the Dutch have had to pay close attention to their land use due to the fact that half of the Netherlands lies only one metre above sea level. To give better perspective to the last statement, note that most countries of the world are well above 200 metres above sea level.

But it is not just the worry about sea levels that helped the Dutch house its poor and middle-income earners; her leadership has historically taken bold and deliberate steps to curb housing deficits. An iterative process of fine-tuning housing policies has always been adopted "to keep pace with the times" in the words of Thomas Jefferson.

The Dutch Housing Acts of 1901, 1947, 1965 and 1993

were enacted and then subsequently replaced to ensure dynamism and relevance. Currently, a new act of 2015 which amongst others, caps possible yearly rent increments, exists in response to a problem in pricing of social housing accommodation. While the Dutch model is definitely not perfect, its responsiveness to creating new policy and also enforcing, it has created visible results that are applauded and emulated worldwide.

The fact is that both the demand and supply of houses are influenced by government policies; a stagnant legal framework for housing would create a stench like murky waters that do not change or flow. So to choose only one word to describe the best housing policies from a list comprising: consistent, coherent, articulate, responsive, powerful, stimulating and dynamic, always opt for dynamic. Dynamic laws change when they are not consistent, coherent, articulate, responsive, powerful or stimulating enough to achieve the expected results.

FOUR

How Housing Policy Determines Housing Affordability

Policies govern every facet of society, including affordable housing. Affordable housing doesn't just exist; governments, through practical and progressive policies, set the stage for housing to be affordable.

Prior to the U.S Tax Reform Act of 1986, only a few developers in the United States undertook affordable housing projects, as these projects usually connoted lower rents than market-rate projects, lower net operating income, and ultimately, lower ROI. As an initiative of the U.S Federal government to close the affordable housing gap and make affordable housing projects financially appealing to real estate developers, the Low-Income Housing Tax Credit (LIHTC) program, often called "lie tech" tax credit, was born out of the Tax Reform Act.

As a Public-Private Partnership between the Federal government, State governments, developers and investors, the LIHTC program was created to attract private money to affordable housing developments. Each state through its Housing Finance Authority (HFA) would allocate Federal Income Tax credits to developers over a ten-year period. In return, the developer would acquire, rehabilitate or construct rental housing for low-income households and operate the project under LIHTC guidelines for a 15-year compliance period.

These developers then sell 'the right to use these tax credits' to investors (which are usually corporations, like banks) looking to reduce their Federal taxes. The investor's capital contribution to the project then reduces the developer's need for other finance sources. This in turn reduces the developer's debt-service cost, allowing the project to be financially attractive with below-market rental income. In 2016, the US Department for Housing and Urban Development (HUD) placed the LIHTC's annual tax credit authorisation at $8Bn. This has led to the realisation of about 2.8M affordable housing units.

A year after Singapore attained self-governance, the Housing and Development Board (HDB) created in 1960 with the task of managing new and existing buildings, clearing and redeveloping slums and urban areas, and developing rural and agricultural areas for resettlement. The HDB team, led by Chairman Lim Kim San, launched its first program – The Five Year Building Programme – which realised 51,031 housing units between 1961 and 1965. About 10,000 low cost flats were then awarded to low-income households. In February 1964, the HDB launched the Home Ownership for the People Scheme. Before this scheme, Singaporeans could only rent apartments built by the HDB. The Home Ownership for the People Scheme allowed low-income earners to buy flats on a 99-year lease at affordable prices from the government. This bridged the gap between affordable, sustainable housing and home ownership.

The Prime Minister at the time believed that social and political stability were dependent on home ownership. The home ownership scheme elevated home ownership over apartment rental, as the HDB allowed households with a monthly income of less than $800 to make monthly payments lower than the open market price of rental flats. In 1968, the Amended Central Provident Fund (CPF) Act was passed to allow citizens to use their CPF to pay for HDB flats. Singaporeans were now able to pay initial deposits and monthly loans with their disposable income along with their CPF savings. About 80% of Singaporeans currently live in Government built flats.

The absence of order is chaos. Laws breed order; and the absence of laws breed disorder. As with the U.S and Singapore, developing nations need to enact policies that will create a pull-factor for affordable housing development.

FIVE

How Government Can Make Land Cheaper Without Reducing Price

Land is very expensive. It amounts to about 25 to 65% of the total cost of developing a single house unit depending on what part of the earth you're standing. Ironically, land is defined as a free gift of nature. Free, yet so expensive, even when property prices stagnate or are reduced, land values seem to always soar.

Governments in different countries hold varied roles with regards to land management; some own all land, some own a portion, while some governments have so liberalised land ownership that they struggle to access the resource.

But one thing almost all governments retain is the power to issue or refuse planning permission for the development of land. Government can use these planning powers to make land less expensive to buyers without reducing the unit price of the land in three distinctly related ways.

Firstly, Government can make land less expensive by reducing setback and building line requirements. Setbacks refer to the distance that a building is located from its boundaries to the street and to neighbouring properties. Take for illustration a parcel of land measuring 600 sqm (30m by 20m) and which costs $1,000 per sqm. This amounts to $600,000. In a country like Nigeria, only about 50% of the land can be developed due to the setback laws (averagely). As such, utility is only derived from 50% of the land in exchange for a value of $600,000. Should the setbacks be reduced by an additional 25%, 75% of the land gives a higher utility but for the same price. This is the case in the UK and several other European countries where a lot of houses are built without any setbacks between them and 1 or 2-metre front setbacks. This amounts to development on up to 80% of land.

Again, governments can reduce the price of land quite similarly by increasing the density of development permissible on plots of land. Where landowners are allowed to develop more than 2 to 3 floors on the average, the cost portion of land to the total development cost diminishes as the development goes higher.

Finally, most parcels of land have a designated land use class. This may be agricultural, residential, commercial, place of worship etc. While such designations are good for giving order to development in towns and cities, planning laws should not be stagnant but should dynamically seek to create a sustainable and serene environment. This may require changing land use as neighbourhoods become gentrified or renewed. By so doing, Government can make land cheaper by re-zoning the use of land to a more viable use. Often times, different uses would pay different prices for land in a particular location. Dynamic zoning laws often permit the use of land for its highest and best use.

Cheaper in the three scenarios described means to increase the value of the land without a corresponding rise in the price the owner pays for it. Should any or all these ideas be implemented in a developing country, prices may rise initially due to pent up demand, but this will soon fizzle out as the new becomes the norm and property values return to being determined primarily by market forces rather than a dynamic move by the government to stimulate development.

SIX

How Government can make renting cheaper without reducing the price

In most countries of the world, the government is the regulator of housing and urban development. This means the government has the powers to create policies that must be adopted by all parties in the housing market, landlords and tenants inclusive.

In some countries, the government agency in charge of housing attempts to lower or regulate rents by issuing rent control laws. Rent controls are aimed at controlling rents to ensure investors, developers and property owners do not charge exorbitant or outrageous prices as rents. In a rent-control law, the fixed rent or range of rent chargeable per location is stated, and everyone is expected to comply. As much as tenants love this, rent controls often end up stifling the housing market – thus discouraging new developments and forcing the emergence of black markets. Unless the government is giving some inducement for landlords to fix their rents, in the long term, rent controls often do not work.

Without reducing, fixing or controlling rents, government can make renting cheaper in three distinct ways.

In most developing countries, like Nigeria and Ghana, where prime rents are high and unaffordable, rents are typically charged annually upfront. In some cases, landlords demand up to two to three years rent in advance! This can be very expensive. Government can make renting cheaper by creating laws mandating monthly rent collections and actively enforcing the law. This immediately makes renting cheaper. To start with, salaries are received monthly in these countries, so an annual tenancy payment does not even match the cash flow of the average occupier. A wider range of properties would become affordable to any individual if rents were charged monthly.

To make monthly rent collections work, Government should implement this second suggestion. Government and all her agencies should model compliance to the monthly-rent-collect laws by only paying monthly rents when renting and demanding monthly rents from government properties. In most countries, government is the biggest landlord. This is understandable as government often has unlimited access to land to develop housing. They often have many more resources than the average private developer to also develop the land for housing. As such, once government starts to model compliance, a significant size of the market will complain, and this forces private landlords to do same, in order to stay competitive.

Finally, the government can make renting cheaper, without reducing price, by reducing property taxes. Occupational and title perfection charges have a fine way of informing how much is charged as rent. Even when this is not the case, most occupiers believe it is, and so it psychologically informs their choice. Should a gazette be issued reducing property taxes, landlords immediately have less financial burdens to transfer to tenants, and tenants also receive the news with joy knowing a reduction will come their way in some shape, form or order. This will, overtime, permeate market dynamics and push prices down, all other major factors being constant.

When taxes are reduced, compliance is higher, so government still earns more – win-win.

SEVEN

How Government can make mortgages cheaper without reducing the price

Houses are expensive capital goods. The median and average price of a US flat and detached house is $313,500 and $377,700 respectively (US Census, September 2016). That is a lot of money, and it is relatively the same story in most parts of the world. Consequently, the average Joe doesn't pay cash down for a home. Since houses ordinarily come with title deeds, this is mortgaged to secure a loan, which typically the buyer cannot really afford.

With an average paying job and many foreseeable working years to go, a working class man should be able to afford a mortgage on a commensurately priced house by simply spreading the payments over a long enough period of time. In most developed countries, this is the case, but in developing or underdeveloped nations, it's not quite so.

The World Bank computes mortgage depth of countries as a percentage of the mortgage loans availed in comparison to the country's GDP. The US has a mortgage depth of 75%; the UK, 83%; Switzerland, 98%; and Denmark a whopping 110%. On the flip side of the spectrum, Ghana, Nigeria, Egypt and Tanzania all have a less than 1% mortgage penetration.

This is not surprising, as Nigeria for example has an average mortgage-lending rate of 24% per annum. Again, the interest charged is not surprising, as banks have to compete for funds with "risk-free" Federal Government bonds – which pay as high as 18%, as against their European counterparts whose Eurobonds have a negative yield.

But irrespective of price: in the Netherlands, which has a mortgage depth of 83%, mortgage loans for first-time home buyers are fully tax deductible for up to 30 years. This means that as long as the house you are buying is your first and primary residence, the government will refund your mortgage interest payments from your personal income tax that is deducted from source and paid by your employer.

This immediately makes mortgages cheaper, irrespective of the price (interest) charged by the bank. So assume a Dutch homebuyer pays 40% of his or her income as tax, and earns 1,000 Euros pre-tax, meaning 600 Euros post-tax. If his bank charges the conventional maximum of 30% of disposable income (post-tax income) as mortgage repayment, this would mean he pays 200 Euros in mortgage repayment. This means the 200 Euros paid as a monthly mortgage repayment would be sufficiently fully refunded from his tax. It is therefore "free" to take a mortgage, and it would be ridiculous not to do so, all other requirements being met.

Should this law be enacted in Nigeria, where the income tax is about 25% of personal income, these would be the statistics: A homebuyer with a post-tax income of 150,000 Naira will pay 50,000 Naira in tax. If he is also charged a maximum of 30% of his income in mortgage repayment, he will be paying 45,000 monthly. Consequently, a fully deductible mortgage policy will just adequately refund his mortgage payment.

This immediately makes mortgages affordable, if not free, to home buyers who can fulfil other conditions such as showing a steady source of income for loan repayment. Now before you jump to the Government's defence on the tax loss it will have to bear, note that such loss will be on a steady decline after an initial period of policy hype and then stabilization.

As people begin to joyfully take up mortgages for first home purchases, this will create significant competition amongst mortgage providers, thus setting in motion the basic laws of economics. Mortgage prices would have to fall to stay competitive, consequently reducing tax refund obligations of the Government over time.

In all, as mortgage prices and tax deductions reduce, mortgage penetration of the adopting country would increase.

EIGHT

The Economic Value of Housing Subsidies

Housing is expensive, and everyone knows this. Without financial help, a good number of people would be homeless. Aside from family and friends, one source most people look to for housing assistance is the government. This is why housing is always a recurring promise by most politicians seeking to get elected…

Housing subsidies are government interventions to help reduce the cost of rental housing or home ownership. They can come in different forms and at varied stages of the housing acquisition process, depending on the reasoning of the government of the day. But like any other type of subsidy, someone has to pay for it; and while many think it is the government that pays, it is the alternative foregone that really pays. Governments are confronted with an unending list of demands, and any avenue that is chosen means that others are not chosen. So any housing subsidies offered must have overcome other demands in some way.

In his 2006 article titled "Million Dollar Murray," published in The New Yorker and later rewritten in his book *What the Dog Saw*, Malcolm Gladwell tells the story of a homeless alcoholic named Murray who was always in and out of the hospital, the jail and the shelters that are all financed by the state. After ten years, the funds the state had spent on the social services that he required had amounted to a million dollars. True story.

But according to Professor Tom Carter of the University of Winnipeg's Institute of Urban Studies, "There is a literature that talks about it [the economic value of social housing] in a general sense, but nothing in terms of dollars and cents. Consequently, we can only be guided more by intuition than evidence." This is also true.

Three additional truths are: First, it is cheaper to subsidize housing than to pay for healthcare if people are homeless. Healthcare is an endeavour that requires the highest level of skill, perhaps because it has to do with human life. Consequently it is very expensive. In addition to the skills and professionals required, research, drugs, machines and various facilities further make healthcare very costly. It is better to be subsidized, to stay indoors and to stay healthy rather than battle diseases that may require lifelong treatment and may be incurable.

Secondly, it is cheaper to subsidize housing than to pay for the incarceration and correction of citizens if they commit crimes when they are homeless. Again, it is intuitive that people are more likely to commit crimes when they are homeless – in a bid to survive or get ahead. But, considering the enormous resources and lengthy value chain that security provision entails, it is easy to see that paying rent for households would be cheaper.

Thirdly, it is cheaper to subsidize housing than to pay for their additional education, feeding and social support if they are too unstable to gain a normal education and earn a living due to homelessness. It is hard to even think of a person of any age successfully attending classes and scoring A's or even C's while being homeless. Education is one activity that requires some level of stability to get it right. But not being educated begins a downward spiral; when a person isn't educated, his/her job opportunities are limited, and if he/she remains unemployed, the state will have to provide support. The alternative – to provide housing at the beginning of the cycle – seems much wiser.

Developed nations understand that it is cheaper to create affordable housing rather than trying to manage homelessness, and that's why they provide or enable social and affordable housing. Developing countries also need to understand this.

NINE

Creative and Sustainable Subsidies for Affordable Housing

When buying or renting a home or developing houses to sell or rent, there are three broad sources of housing finance possibly available: equity, debt and subsidies. Whenever the term subsidy is mentioned, what easily comes to mind is the government or a philanthropist doling out cash. But subsidies can and should be more sophisticated than a sporadic free pass. To be sustainable, governments need to adopt creative means of helping people afford homes.

This can be approached from the supply side – subsidizing the development of affordable homes; and also from the demand side – subsidizing the buying or renting of affordable homes.

To subsidise the development of affordable homes, governments can part-finance the housing creation process, which involves: obtaining permits, logistics, construction and maintenance. At each stage, subsidies or waivers can be granted to reduce total development costs. Affordable housing developers may be granted tax holidays, tax caps or tax waivers to further promote the affordability cause. Similarly, they may be given low-priced loans, insurance or financial guarantees in order to obtain loans.

A different method would be to create an enabling environment for affordable housing developments to exist and to thrive. For instance, governments may cross-subsidize affordable housing by granting planning permission for certain commercial developments in exchange for a portion being affordable housing or else land where affordable homes can be developed. Similarly, land value capture is sometimes used – when governments grant landowners or developers permission to develop more densely on their land by reducing setbacks; or to increase building height limits; or to rezone the land to a more viable use. In return for this permission, which substantially increases the value of the land, the developers either provide land for affordable housing or build the units.

On the demand side, governments may indirectly enable demand or directly provide subsidies that grant citizens access to affordable housing. Urban renewals and development of mass transit systems in new towns help make housing more affordable by making transportation and other social amenities available and cheaper to access. Rent controls, lower mortgage rates, tax deductible mortgages, housing allowances, and free or subsidised utilities all directly improve access to affordable homes.

In 2016, the U.S government offered $30 billion in rental subsidies for low-income housing and spent almost $6 billion on public social housing, which significantly helped to bridge the country's housing shortage. Such schemes in the U.S. have been in effect since the 1930's at the time of President Franklyn Roosevelt. Developing countries also need to step in with creative subsidies to help house low-income families when their standard equity or debt limits are overstretched.

TEN

Unlocking Land: Who holds the key?

L and is the bedrock of all production. With respect to developing affordable housing, it represents about 20 to 60 percent of costs and is usually the starting point for any such project. And it is often the biggest challenge.

In 2014, the McKinsey Global Institute published "A blueprint for addressing the global affordable housing challenge." The report identified four cost-reduction levers for affordable housing. The first lever proposes unlocking land for affordable housing through channels such as transit-oriented development, initiating idle-land policies, land pooling, and releasing public land.

Developing affordable housing in a "transit-oriented" manner is non-negotiable for sustainability. Affordable housing is needed most by low income earners who commonly do not own cars and who work in low-paying jobs at CBDs or main commercial centres. As such, affordable housing located more than one hour away from work kicks in a new financial strain due to higher transportation costs, making it both unsuitable and unsustainable. Similarly, it's critical to consider major transit facilities when locating affordable housing projects. It's important to resist the temptation to locate affordable housing in the cheapest locations if they are hours away from major transport infrastructure and from centres of commerce.

Interestingly, most cities still have a good amount of undeveloped and idle land that can be made available for affordable housing through idle land policies. Such policies entail local authorities offering incentives for developing idle land within a certain timeframe, and/or issuing penalties for non-development of land within a certain timeframe. The Lagos state government in Nigeria has often stimulated property development through issuance of penalties for non-development within a certain timeframe. In such cases, non-complying undeveloped land can be legally confiscated and then made available for affordable housing projects because they were obtained at a relatively low price.

In certain instances, owners of adjoining fragmented, underused land or run-down properties may be unable to adequately utilise their individual properties due to poor accessibility, unavailability of infrastructure, or other restrictions. The owners may pool their properties together to receive smaller plot sizes proportionate to their stake in the pool. In exchange, the portion given up by the owners can be disposed to finance the needed infrastructure improvement.

Governments of most countries tend to be the biggest landholders and can help unlock urban land for affordable housing by releasing land tracts under their control specifically for affordable housing. In Turkey, TOKI – a government-housing agency – has contributed the equivalent of four percent of urban land in Turkey into partnerships with private developers for development of affordable housing under a revenue-sharing arrangement. TOKI has a vision of providing one million housing units by 2023, 40% of which are slated to be social housing.

So the code to unlocking land for affordable housing is not so much about 'who holds the key?' but more about 'what is the key?' There are a few keys that can unlock land, depending on their appropriateness for each business case.

ELEVEN

The Most Important P In PPPs

Public Private Partnerships seem to have come full circle. Though some form of PPPs have been seen dating back to the Roman Empire in the 14th century, PPPs as we know it garnered a lot of hype in the 1970's and reached a high with a lot of developments successfully taking off by adopting the PPP model. However, as with most "shooting-star-type" ideas, it soon reached a hiatus and then PPP transactions slowed. Over the years, as some projects experienced murky waters or outright failed, PPPs left a hangover, which has now led to a period of hindsight where both researchers and practitioners are looking more carefully at the model to see what works or what does not work before adopting PPPs to finance infrastructure deficits.

A cursory reflection on the model shows that it's the last "P" in PPPs that makes a world of difference. The model might as well be tagged "local-international partnerships" or "government-professionals partnerships." It is the last word

– Partnerships – inferring collaboration and a distribution of responsibilities between two or more entities – that truly makes the model successful. Where one party views the other as a vendor or contractor rather than a partner, the model is much more likely to not be effective. Also, where a party views itself as the subject-matter-expert, and the counterpart as an ignoramus that can be exploited, the experts may as well be engaged as consultants. And that means losing the third "P."

Partnerships infer the laying down of weaknesses and inefficiencies by one party under the symbiotic concealment of the strengths and resources of the other party to the benefit of all. Such vulnerability and clarity of roles is typically present in the best-performing PPPs.

PPPs hold significant horizontal and vertical integration benefits. Vertical integration refers to the integration of different responsibilities along the value chain to optimize life cycle cost, while horizontal integration pertains to the expansion of specific responsibilities to optimize the interface and existing competency. However, for such benefits to be mined, parties have to be fully committed, rational, and open in their approach to the partnership. It's not the type of parties that matter (private or/and public); it's the full agreement to partner under the agreed terms that is important.

In adopting PPPs to provide affordable housing, it's easy to see two scenarios that don't lead to a successful project. On one hand, a developer/financier-led project may result in the development of housing that's well built but too closely priced to commercial prices and therefore not affordable.

On the other hand, a public-sector-led project may result in affordable houses that are not well built. In this scenario, one factor that may result in poor quality is if the private sector entity ensures he maintains his commercial profitability by cutting corners with design and materials.

Both scenarios above attest to a PPP that does not fully consider what both parties will earn for their contributions and how they will ensure their sufficiency. Government cannot expect a private company to enter a PPP aimed at selling houses for less than market value when the developer/financier has to pay market value for all the inputs of the project. On the other hand, government is in a position to ensure that the private entity gets tax breaks, or lower financing, or free/inexpensive land, or possibly other advantages – in order to ensure that the final output is affordable while the developer still earns decently for the effort. At the same time, the private sector cannot expect that – having obtained so much help from the government – the final product will be sold at market prices. That would be overkill.

In any kind of partnership, if you do not fully ensure that what enters your partner's pocket is commensurate with their effort and that they will be satisfied, you may be setting yourself up for a transaction that will go bust down the line.

PART 2
// THE PRIVATE SECTOR

TWELVE

Laissez Faire

On a memorable day in 1681, the French Minister of Finance met with leading French businessmen, seeking their advice on how the government could improve the French economy. Their response was "Laissez nous faire" which translates to "Leave it to us." The French businessmen were not exactly asking the government to leave the economy in the hands of the men in the room; they were essentially asking the government to stay its powers to intervene, subsidize or control market forces.

The private sector is very powerful, and often more efficient than government. Efficiency refers to using less to get more. Private organizations, unlike governments, must seek to be efficient for two major reasons. First, they do not have unlimited resources. If they are going to be profitable, they must maximise income and minimise costs. Secondly, private organisations are faced with competition. To retain customers, they have to beat or get ahead of the competition.

Often times the responsibility or the capability to develop affordable housing is relegated to the government. But if the private sector is more efficient; if they can thrive despite limited resources, doesn't that sound like they are best positioned to deliver on affordable housing?

That is the situation in the Netherlands, where the social housing program, which houses over 30 percent of the Dutch urban population, is run by a highly organised private-sector-led social housing system. There are about 360 social housing companies, which in the Netherlands are called social housing associations (SHAs). They own a 2.4 million rental housing stock, which houses about 4 million of the Netherlands' 17 million people. As of 2016, 44% of new residential constructions in the Netherlands were social housing dwellings. The SHA's also own and manage special care housing, student housing and sustainability facilities.

These social housing associations are private organisations with a public task. Their core responsibilities are spelled out in the Social Housing Management Decree which strives to: assure good quality in all homes; rent on a priority basis to the special attention groups; involve tenants in the management of the organisation; make a contribution to the quality of life in communities; and contribute to the housing of persons in need of care.

The activities of these privately run social housing associations are supervised by an umbrella body, and all SHA's belong to it. It is known as the Dutch Association of Social Housing Organisations or 'Aedes'. Social housing associations' rent charges per location are determined through a point-based system and guided by the Dutch national rent policy, which shows maximum annual increases and permissible rents in all parts of the country. On average, SHA's charge about 72% of the maximum rent spelled out in the rent policy, while commercial rents are, on average, about 80% of the stipulated rent cap.

The Dutch affordable housing system has its own issues, but it is acclaimed as one of the best in the world. Despite being private sector led, and having financial and administrative autonomy from the government, it is efficient and publicly impactful. "Leave it to us," the French businessmen said of the French economy. "Leave it to them," the Dutch government said of affordable housing.

THIRTEEN

Public Problem, Private Sector Opportunity

According to McKinsey, the affordable housing gap as a percentage of the GDP of Lagos and Mumbai is 15% and 10% respectively, which are some of the highest in the world. This statistic shows both a problem and an opportunity. It demonstrates that the value of affordable housing required in Lagos amounts to about 15% of the state's GDP; but it also infers that the market size available to a private affordable housing developer is about 15% of the GDP of Lagos. This is just one of the many opportunities that affordable housing development holds for private sector participants.

The UK Homes and Communities Agency showed that social housing associations invested over £5.4 billion in new housing properties in 2016 alone; completed 42,000 social homes; and made an operating surplus/income of £4.8 billion. Their Dutch counterparts, according to the

IPD Netherlands Annual Social Housing Index, saw annual returns rise to 10.1%, up from 8% one year prior. The performance of these well developed social housing markets attest to the potential of venturing into low-cost housing enterprises.

Should private sector developers in developing countries awaken to the opportunities affordable housing development offers, it would create unprecedented growth in the local construction market. The magnitude of construction scale required to solve the affordable housing challenges in most developing countries, if addressed, will not go unnoticed in their GDP computations. A boom in construction activities will create many jobs and generally stimulate economic prosperity.

Affordable housing also delivers an opportunity for the finance sector. Financing will be needed by affordable housing developers in the form of construction loans, bridge financing, and other financial products such as bank guarantees. Mortgages will be needed to fund purchases of new affordable housing by the eventual users, if it is priced adequately.

At the heart of the matter is the fact that providing affordable housing in the right locations heightens a city's productivity by integrating lower-income residents into the economy. This has a far-reaching impact, ranging from improved living standards to reduction in crime rates. For large institutions and small businesses in any location with increased affordable housing, the target market for products and services is boosted and everyone wins.

While affordable housing can sometimes pose a public problem, it definitely creates a myriad of private opportunities.

FOURTEEN

Highest Bidder or Highest Needer

One of the major problems of the world is the non-existence of a middle ground when it comes to most ideologies. It must be black or white, and having grey will be an adulteration of both, which is typically not palatable to either party. But what if it could be both white and black? Two men standing on each side of a figure written in the sand may see 6 or 9, depending on what side they stand, but if they move to the middle, they only need to look left and right, and perhaps twist their neck awkwardly, to see that it's both 6 and 9. So to truly have the best of middle grounds, you only need to know where and when to turn.

Developers are the lead catalysts for housing provision. A Developer is the entity that assembles all other parties and requirements necessary to provide homes. For all this effort, they desire to be, and should be, well compensated. On the other hand, housing is a benefit that should be enjoyed by all. Housing should not always be offered to the highest bidder but should be made accessible to the people that need it most.

For housing to be sustainably provided – that is, to reach those who need it, and not just benefit speculators – developers must not stand on either side of commercial or social, but must move to the middle ground and determine under which parameters homes will be built to cater to the highest bidder or highest 'needer'.

Fully commercial developers sell or let to whomever walks in through the door and pays the highest. In a booming economy, speculators will walk in first and with the most cash, thereby driving prices to a point that is no longer sustainable for even the developers. On the flip side, social developers will attempt to sell to the poorest – the sub-prime and the needy. Unfortunately, they may not make good enough returns to keep in business and repeat the development cycle long enough to wipe out the housing deficit. This is often the case with public development corporations that attempt to provide homes at cost or less; the programme is eventually unsustainable and runs out of resources to continue.

The middle is the key. The middle is where private developers with a social mandate develop housing projects for a decent profit and target the acquisition at those who truly need the homes. These two aspects must be carefully curated – the construction and the disposal (sale or lease).

Where the construction process is too expensive or

wasteful, the final product becomes too expensive for the target market. Also, where the target market is not carefully identified, speculators will infiltrate the process, seeking to purchase for cheap something that they will flip in the near future at higher values. At this point, the resolve, resourcefulness and restrictions that the developer has, will determine the success of the project. And success will be defined as an affordable housing project being delivered to those who need affordable homes to live in.

This was the case with Alejandro Aravena – a Chilean architect and the founder of Elemental – a for-profit business with a social interest. Alejandro and his team worked creatively within the subsidy budget of a group of 100 families to develop homes for them on a 5,000 sqm site in the city centre. The initial conventional design options only allowed for either 30 or 62 homes to be built on the relatively small site. The final project – Quinta Monroy – was a development of 100 row houses with each house covering just 72sqm, and with options for incremental development up to an additional 50% area as the finances of each family improved. The project required resolve, resourcefulness, and restrictions added by Elemental, in order to ensure that the goal was achieved. The project has received worldwide acclaim, and Alejandro won awards for sustainable construction and also the Priktzer Architecture Prize, amongst many others.

FIFTEEN

A Different Kind of Exclusivity

In developing countries like Nigeria and Ghana, a number of property developers casually classify their developments as affordable housing projects, often times because the project is priced relatively lower than median house prices in the region. But merely reducing initial sale prices does not accurately classify a project as an affordable housing project. Sale price reductions may make for a good marketing and differentiation strategy, but they do not make the project really affordable. Affordable housing projects require a different kind of exclusivity.

For a project to be truly affordable, there must be a selection process for buyers or renters. If a development is available to anyone who can afford it, with little or no restrictions on entry and exit, it is not an affordable housing project. The entry price may be affordable, but Speculators will snap it up quickly at the "cheap" starting prices and then offer the same houses for sale at more commercial prices in the near future.

At this point, no one may even remember that the project was meant to be an affordable housing project. .

Affordable housing is in high demand but it should not be sold to the highest bidder. There must be a method for selecting those who access it fairly. Equity and fairness are watchwords of developers who seek to reduce homelessness and improve home ownership. Only those buyers who cannot afford commercially-priced projects should be allowed to set foot on the affordable housing ladder. It's the equitable thing to do. This can be done through various methods, including the creation of wait lists, lotteries, or adopting pre-determined demographic criteria such as age, sex or physical disability. In all cases, income level is a base criterion to ensure wealthier people do not access affordable homes to the detriment of poorer individuals and families.

This is the case in many developed countries. In the United States, the Department for Housing and Urban Development and its sub-agencies are responsible for ensuring that only those who are properly pre-qualified, based on income level and other parameters, get on the affordable housing waitlist and eventually get to rent or buy an affordable home. In Massachusetts, an Affordability Monitoring Handbook is published as a guide for accessibility to affordable housing. In the UK, the Homes and Communities Agency plays a similar role and makes it possible for First Time Buyers within certain income brackets to access social, affordable or intermediate housing schemes.

Aside from exclusive selection processes based on fair and pre-defined criteria, affordable housing projects need to have transfer restrictions to maintain prices and ownership over time. These restrictions on transfer act to ensure that the projects remain affordably priced, rather than being sold or rented to the highest bidder. Designated government agencies in developed countries help to monitor the resale, sublease, and any other form of transfer of affordable houses, even when the properties are bought or rented from private companies. These agencies serve as watchdogs against speculators and other individuals who may want to cheat the system and allow commercial prices to inform transfers.

Affordability requires a different kind of exclusivity: selection and restrictions as essential levers to ensure sustained affordability.

SIXTEEN

Affordable Finance for Affordable Housing

The British government expends millions of pounds every year on art, culture and heritage. This funds the acquisition of art and antiques, cultural events, and construction and maintenance of state-owned museums, galleries, theatres, parks and heritage sites that are visited freely or affordably by both citizens and foreigners every day. Aside from the jobs created, and also the tourism, public aesthetics, and pride that these civic sites and features create, one might begin to wonder why the government "wastes" such enormous funds on them.

For many years, this sort of expenditure had been a drain on the British treasury, and Prime Minister Winston Churchill was directed by the Crown to cut expenditure on art and heritage – which he refused to do. So alongside expenditures like free healthcare and subsidised education, the British government found an affordable way to finance these ventures – the national lottery. Since 1994, when the program was launched, the UK has successfully raised over 50 billion pounds from the national lottery to fund various causes. Forty per cent of the government's income from the national lottery was spent on art and heritage in the year ending 31 March 2017.

Financial institutions are in the business of taking calculated and lower risks for the highest returns they can get. Consequently, they do not necessarily want to lend to lower income brackets who are the primary recipients of affordable housing. When they do, the rates are increased to account for the perceived increase in risk; and this may make an affordable housing project become unaffordable for the end-user.

To make mortgage financing affordable for buyers of affordable housing projects, housing finance institutions need to make appropriate changes to lower interest rates, much like the UK matching lottery earnings to finance art and culture spending.

The first point of call would be to revisit how mortgages are funded. Tenured deposits, commercial papers, and other fixed income issuances tend to attract high costs and are short term in comparison to mortgages. As such, from a price and duration perspective, they are a mismatch for affordable housing loans.

Mortgages are better financed through core savings deposits, which are the lowest priced financial products in any financial market. Better yet, a secondary mortgage provider who can buy mortgage loans from the primary housing finance institutions at lower rates can be considered. While developed countries have successfully established such secondary operators, attempts at this are yet to effectively reduce rates in developing countries like Ghana and Nigeria.

Another category of change needed to make housing finance cheaper is to reduce loan origination costs. This can be done by improving the methods used in assessing and prequalifying borrowers. More efficient processes that reduce administrative costs and overheads would eventually translate to lower lending rates. Also, property valuations, which are required to determine the value of the house to be mortgaged, can sometimes be time-consuming and expensive. Introducing standardized property valuation methods would reduce both time and cost.

Progressive and out-of the-box thinking is required to hack affordable mortgages. Like the British who so cherish culture and found a way to finance it unrelatedly through lotteries, housing finance professionals can engineer new ways to ensure low-income earners experience financial inclusion.

SEVENTEEN

The Five C's Of Housing Loans

The five C's of credit have become popular as the broad reasons a loan is approved or not. They incorporate both qualitative and quantitative factors in assessing a borrower's suitability for a loan. Generally, most creditors will not view housing loans particularly differently from other forms of credit, as housing loans are actually a significant percentage of bank loan portfolios. As such, the five C's of credit are the five C's of housing loans. The C's are the same, but how creditors really see them is the big difference.

Character
The character of the borrower is known by his/her track record or reputation. Where available, the credit history is called up to show the past credit performance of the intending borrower, and this is used to adjudge future performance. Proxies for credit history may vary from location to location, but information on a loan applicant's financial discipline and history is perhaps the first consideration in determining

if a housing loan will be granted or otherwise.

Capacity

The capacity of a borrower to repay the loan is a major consideration for lenders. This is primarily assessed by the income and employment status/history of the intending borrower. The length of time the borrower has been at his/her present job helps confirm the stability of his/her income. Another consideration is the existence of other loans the borrower may be servicing; most housing loan providers will need sufficient comfort that such existing repayment obligations will not hinder the repayment of the loan under review. For housing loans, the rule of thumb is that 30% of the borrower's monthly income should adequately cover the estimated monthly repayment. Where this is the case, the borrower is safely said to have capacity.

Capital

Part of how Warren Buffet assesses if a company has good and committed management worthy of his investment is, as he coined it, if the management team has "skin in the game." You are less likely to default on your obligations when your own money has also been invested in the venture. In similar fashion, housing loan financiers demand that borrowers make a down payment for mortgage or construction loans alike. The portion of down payment required may vary by location, but this rule stands true and veritable.

Conditions

Conditions are two-prong. On the one hand, the conditions of a loan refer to the loan terms such as interest rates and fees chargeable, loan tenure, and other terms which may allow a lender to grant a loan to a particular loan applicant or not. On the other hand, it also refers to the purpose to which the loan will be put. For housing loans, such purpose is usually to buy land, construct on land, or buy an already built house. Typically, financiers prefer to finance loans for a specific purpose, which provides better transparency and perhaps more clarity on the source of repayment. Often times, loans may be disapproved because the conditions under which the lender will be willing to lend may not be suitable to the loan applicant. For example, a lender who only grants 20-year mortgages may not be able to grant a mortgage to a 60-year-old man, while another lender who grants 5-year mortgages may be willing to deal.

Collateral
Collateral is an asset that is pledged as security for a loan, and in the event of default it is sold to repay the debt. This is a major requirement of most financiers; unsecured loans are getting harder to come by. This loan requirement is often favourable to housing loans as housing loans are typically obtained to acquire an asset – either land or housing. As such, the loan would simply be secured by the asset to be acquired. This, however, means that the property must have good and secure title for the loan.

Where a borrower has sufficient capital and collateral, demonstrates character and capacity, meets and is also willing to accept the conditions for a loan, he will have scaled the high walls of housing loans.

EIGHTEEN

Higher Value For Money

The term 'affordable housing' is defined and described in various ways, depending on who's doing the narration and where. But 'UN-Habitat' broadly defines affordable housing as "that which is reasonably adequate in standard and location for a lower- and middle-income occupant(s) and does not cost so much that it prohibits the occupant(s) meeting other basic living costs or threatens their enjoyment of basic human rights." This definition is widely accepted and quoted, partly because the definition resonates with the average listener as a fair depiction of the concept.

Looking carefully at this description, a few inferences can be drawn. Firstly, affordable housing doesn't infer sub-standard houses in remote locations. That a house is affordable does not mean it has to be the worst house available on the market. Secondly, affordable housing is very cost-centric, seeking out homes for less than average market value. It is this that actually defines a house as being affordable – price.

The price has to be low enough to ensure that the occupant can meet other basic living costs and enjoy the basic human rights that life has to offer.

In any business or economic transaction, what the receiving party essentially seeks is value for money. You enter a grocery store and exchange a dollar bill for a Snickers bar; you expect to receive a packaged snack with milk chocolate, crunchy nuts and caramel, and anything short of this is a rip-off. Value for money can mean either attaining a higher quality level at the same price, or receiving the same quality level for less money. Either way, subscribers want an efficient and effective product: a widget that meets objectives using fewer resources, and one that meets objectives sooner.

The value for money concept partly describes affordable housing. There is no set price limit that makes a house affordable or not; what is important is that it provides higher value for money. This can be either by attaining a higher quality level at a lower price, or by offering the same quality level for much less money than what is ordinarily available on the market. Simply put, affordable houses give much more value for money than commercially available houses.

Let's say that an average 3-bedroom apartment of about 120sqm floor plate, in your choice location, ordinarily sells for circa $100,000. How would you describe a well-built 3-bedroom apartment in your choice location that is being offered for $60,000? I guess you would describe it as affordable. Or perhaps a steal! This is because the property offers higher value for the money.

This shows the relativity of affordable housing as a concept.

It's a moving target that varies from location to location and transaction to transaction. Affordable housing developers need to tweak their financing, construction techniques, spatial utilization, and labour size, among other things, to ensure they can offer a property "which is reasonably adequate in standard and location" for a lower price. This is achieved by applying technology, ingenuity, and, where available, government and community support to offer higher value for money.

NINETEEN

PPP's – The Perfect Blend

The Panama Canal is one of the seven wonders of the modern world – an integral conduit for international trade. The canal is a 77km passage that connects the Pacific Ocean to the Atlantic; Asia to the Americas. When the canal was originally opened in 1914, America had expended a total of $375 million in construction, legal rights and other costs, not counting the tens of thousands of lives lost during construction. It was the most expensive U.S. construction project at the time.

Today, technological, policy and financing innovations exist that would reduce the burden on any one nation taking on a project of such global significance and one that requires enormous capital.

Public Private Partnership (PPP) is a major innovation that can unlock private co-funding of public projects. But adopting PPP's for affordable housing is no easy feat.

Like getting water from a rock, it may be difficult; but if successful it can offer refreshing results. Collaborations between public land-holding authorities and private capital have the potential to produce housing projects that have the prescribed blend of government socialist perspectives and the private value-for-money paradigm.

Take, for example, Pennyville, an affordable and social housing project located southwest of Johannesburg and developed through a public-private-partnership between Calgro group, Absa Bank and the City of Johannesburg. The project is being developed in phases and will, upon completion, comprise a mix of 2,800 social, affordable and open market houses, with 200 homes already built and occupied. In addition to the development of homes, the project includes the construction of infrastructure linkages consisting of roads, power, water and sewage. A major achievement of the project is its successful decongestion of the Zamimpilo township, which is one of Johannesburg's most notorious urban slums.

In Milan, Italy, Cenni di Cambiamento (House of Change) is the largest timber constructed housing project in Europe. The social housing project was completed in 2013 and was a PPP between the Municipality of Milan as landowners, FIL1 as financiers, and Fondazione Housing Sociale as the social and technical advisor. The project consists of 122 housing units, has won several awards, and was built using ethical funds and the design support of the Department of Architecture and Planning of the Polytechnic of Milan.

Then there is the Casa Heiw (House of Harmony) in Little Tokyo, Los Angeles – California is yet another veritable illustration of the blessings of PPPs. The 100-unit affordable housing project is the first of its kind, a modern, beautiful, and truly harmonious home to return to for a low-income earner. Households earning less than 60% of the median income in the neighbourhood qualify for units with reduced rent. Casa Heiw is one of the many affordable housing projects developed by the Little Tokyo Community Development Center in partnership with the California Equity Fund and the National Equity Fund.

Housing development of any kind is capital intensive. Affordable housing is even more challenging, considering that the "affordability" component creates limitations on earnable returns. Innovation entails applying better solutions to meeting objectives, and PPPs may just be the perfect blend for affordable housing.

TWENTY

Learning from Maboneng

In 1994, when the apartheid curtain fell in South Africa, the world watched with joy the making of history – the emergence of a multiracial democracy birthed in Africa's biggest economy. But very quickly, this liberation led to post-apartheid inefficiencies, such as the white flight that emanated in the nation's inner cities, which would lead to the emergence of new nodes like Sandton and the decay of the old urban centres.

Over twenty years later, more than a hundred office, residential and industrial buildings have been "hijacked" by armed gangs who either chased out the white property owners or simply took advantage of the vacuum created when the legitimate owners fled. These neighbourhoods and properties are now havens for crime, prostitution and drug abuse, as the gangs act as enforcers who lease out the un-serviced space to the poor at significantly less-than-market rents.

Prior to the 1990's, Blacks could not live in these urban centres due to the prejudices spelt out in the 1923 Native Urban Areas Act and the strict enforcement of segregation laws that ensured that no coloured person could access such prime property. But in 2008, a 23-year-old property developer decided to do something about this. He figured the inner city still held the soul and culture of Johannesburg, unlike the more shiny and contemporary private developments that dotted the new mid- to high-income suburbs. Working on one property at a time, which quickly scaled to over forty, he "transformed" the buildings in a select precinct of downtown Joburg into a modern, artsy and exciting live-work-and-play zone. This precinct is now known as "Maboneng" (City of Light in Sotho). The area has now attracted many indigenous retail brands, art galleries, and museums, as well as offices and residences for corporates, entrepreneurs, artists, and other creatives and urbanites.

Maboneng is now a popular story of successful urban regeneration, as the area enjoys much better patronage than the other areas in the CBD that are less secure, and also better patronage than the shinier and newer Johannesburg suburbs that pay less attention to culture and indigenous design.

Jonathan Leibmann, CEO of Propertuity, really went out on a limb in redeveloping Maboneng. He didn't have to create a project that would create significant social change and become a location of national pride. But he did. He could have developed more easily in Sandton, Ranburg, Rosebank, or some other mid to high-income location in South Africa. But that wouldn't have transformed South

Africa in such far-reaching ways as did the redevelopment of the Maboneng Precinct.

Across Africa and in other developing countries, developers like Jonathan Leibmann are in high demand – developers who will make significant private profit while delivering commensurate public value are the true architects of rapid growth.

In the words of Jonathan Leibmann in his 2011 TEDx talk at Stellenbosh: "My call to property developers across Africa is to identify the needs of yourselves and those around you, and to see potential in the dilapidated and vacant buildings and transform them to spaces that inspire ideas."

The lesson is to identify not only your needs but also the needs of those around you.

PART 3
// THE PROFESSIONALS

TWENTY-ONE

Heart and Head

Why bother?

That's what any rational person might ask an affordable housing developer in a developing country. Affordable housing development requires at least twice as much thoughtfulness and vigour as regular housing development in order to ensure the suitability of design, funding, construction methodology and buyer/occupier selection so that the scheme is truly affordable and reaches its target market.

So why bother?

In a developing country, a sizeable percentage of the housing demand would not live in an affordable housing scheme due to family size, location preferences, and primarily income levels. A good number of people requiring housing, even in a developing country, are not necessarily confined by affordability but rather by supply, and it's a function of timing to enter the market. So affordability is not the issue; many can still afford housing at commercial prices.

So really, why bother?

Those who bother with affordable housing developments are drawn primarily by passion. They do not have to be social entrepreneurs or non-profits, but they are drawn to meeting a serious need as a profession. Affordable housing requires both the heart and the head; the passion and the profession. The heart continually fuels the head with a special lubricant to ride on over the biggest bumps and through the deepest ditches. Without this, a typical professional would give up, take the easy road and develop for commercial buyers.

They have to bother.

Because very few have the high calling and skill to be affordable housing developers. There are different segments of every market, and different providers cater to the different segments. Just imagine if every hotel was a Marriot or Hilton, every restaurant a Jamie Oliver, every clothing shop a Gucci. Travelodge, MacDonalds, Primark, and the like play a critical role in providing goods and services to the lower-end segments of their various markets. Housing is no different, and the affordable housing developers need not be less profitable if they are skilled at what they do.

If you bother?

Broadly speaking, affordable housing developers may need to exert twice the effort in a bid to keep costs down, but they do not make twice the profit. They will need to go through the rigour of selecting buyers/occupiers carefully to ensure they are not disposing to speculators. They will have to be experts at construction and financial management at the same time. They will need to do so much more but will not earn much more. The good news, however, is that they will always be in demand. They can be likened to defensive stocks – yields may not be high, but they are constant and stable.

Heart and Head
Many affordable housing developers in developed countries are bankrupt or have been forcefully nationalised. Passion is clearly not enough to be an affordable housing developer. There is good reason why most developers are commercial – the alternative (affordable housing) is no easy fry. In every endeavour, sustainability is paramount, and this is where skill comes in to play. Unfortunately, many socialist-minded entrepreneurs dabble in affordable housing with lots of huff and puff, genuinely seeking to disrupt the housing landscape for good. But like a lit candle, they are quickly smothered upon the arrival of strong winds, as affordable housing requires a blend of both heart and head to be sustainably successful.

TWENTY-TWO

Creative Leadership for Affordable Housing

Everything rises and falls on leadership, including developing affordable housing. Vision, passion and capacity for execution are non-negotiable traits (among others) that are required to successfully develop housing projects that are affordable to buy and to live in. Such projects are led by creative entrepreneurs, professionals and teams that are willing and able to think outside the box or expand the box to allow them to achieve their goals.

Kevin Daly Architects (KDA), led by Kevin Daly, is one such organisation. Established in 1991, the firm is a multiple award-winning architecture and development practice based in Los Angeles. They carry out research-led projects by creating communities for education, the arts and dwellings. The firm is also well known for transforming basic urban sites and generic buildings into model communities. This has earned Kevin Daly Architects over thirty AIA awards, the Rudy Bruner Foundation's Gold Medal for Urban Excellence, and LA's Firm of the Year Award. KDA's projects have been featured in publications like The New York Times, The LA Times, Newsweek, Time, Metropolis, and Architectural Record, amongst others.

One of KDA's most notable affordable housing projects is 'Broadway Housing' – a low-income housing project in Santa Monica that is both economical and environmentally sustainable.

Based on the integrated design and smart planning adopted, all 33 housing units do not have air-conditioning, yet remain a comfortable temperature all through the year. This sort of creativity not only makes the houses affordable to buy, but also affordable to live in.

Pocket Living in London is also a developer with a difference. The company sells houses strictly to first-time homebuyers resident in London at a price at least 20% less than surrounding market values. Coupled with the quality of build it offers, this price reduction means affordability without sacrificing quality for London's young urbanites.

Pocket Living achieves this price point by leveraging design, construction technology and legal controls to ensure that the homes are affordable and stay affordable. The company is run by a dynamic team of Chartered Surveyors,

Accountants, Finance experts, IT professionals, Architects, Urban Planners and Construction experts.

In Nigeria, Fibre – a property brokerage company led by Obinna Okwodu – is successfully helping young people rent homes in Africa's biggest city – Lagos. Obinna and his team have hacked how to rent out homes to Lagos urbanites on a monthly basis as opposed to the standard one or two years upfront that is currently prevalent in the city. This seemingly simple switch in rental tenure has made housing much more affordable and accessible to young people who earn wages on a monthly basis, thereby matching a monthly lease structure.

In less than two years, Fibre has leased out over 200 rooms across Lagos, housing over 150 young people and creating a waitlist of over 4,000 verified young tenants seeking homes to rent on a pay-monthly basis.

Creativity requires courage – courage to break from the norm in order to achieve positive results in new ways. This is the sort of leadership required to achieve affordable housing.

TWENTY-THREE

Affordable And Not Horrible

In her book, The Language of Houses, Alison Lurie, an American writer and winner of the Pulitzer Prize, holds that "Every building's architecture affects human beings differently, but what is at the heart of that affection for beautiful buildings and the disdain for ugly ones is a universal language."

This is so true. Neuroesthetics is a branch of neuroscience that studies the sensual basis for the appreciation of artistic endeavours, such as music, art, architecture, or any other creation by aesthetic perception. The existence of this field of study confirms the reality of this "universal language." Indeed, the architecture of beautiful buildings can make us cheerful and happy, but ugly ones can make us sad and melancholy.

In a bid to achieve affordability, design and aesthetics should never be ignored. Houses ought to be a place where children and parents gladly retire to daily after work, play or learning. It is therefore paramount that the home exudes joy and peace. Irrespective of personal architectural preferences – whether classic or contemporary, ancient or modern – a beautiful building is a joy to all, just as an ugly one repels.

Unfortunately, most people, including home designers, think a beautiful building has to be expensive. Clearly, with an open budget, a lot of architects may be able to take a stab at creating a masterpiece, but beauty can also be achieved economically.

Walmer Link is a gated, privately developed, residential community that comprises 29 apartment blocks amounting to a total of 347 accommodation units in Port Elizabeth, South Africa. Walmer Link is simply beautiful. But it is also affordable. More accurately, it is partly social rental housing and partly affordable housing available for outright purchase. The social housing development portion was funded by government subsidies available for social rental housing developments, while the affordable housing portion was financed by the Finance Linked Individual Subsidy Programme (FLISP). Consequently, the selling prices of houses at Walmer Link are lower than comparable properties available in the townships. Yet this affordable development is a celebrated beauty, having won a regional award for architecture in the Eastern Cape.

Similarly, Bayview Hills Gardens in San Francisco is both

an affordable housing project and stunningly attractive. The project comprises 73 green homes specifically targeted at youths formerly in foster care and families who were formerly homeless. The project won the 'affordable residential real estate deal of the year 2014' in San Francisco. The building was previously a derelict motel and criminal hideout. Bayview Hills is very artsy and very green, and is funded through collaboration with civic-minded community members and organizations.

As another example, Lilac Groove in Leeds is described as the UK's first affordable ecological cohousing project. Lilac is an acronym for Low Impact Living Affordable Community, founded by a Leeds University geography lecturer – Dr. Paul Chatterton – and a few others, with a mission to create eco-friendly and affordable homes. The homes were built using a new low-carbon construction technology called ModCell. The method uses straw and timber to create super-insulated wall panels. The project suffered a prolonged delay in execution, primarily due to funding, which was provided by the co-housing members. In the end, a multi-award-winning minimalist and green housing development that houses twenty happy households was the result.

Walmer Link, Bayview Hills and Lilac Groove, along with a myriad of other architecturally pleasing affordable housing projects that dot the landscapes of cities and towns all across the world, prove that affordable housing can be both affordable and beautiful.

TWENTY-FOUR

Small but Sufficient

The i10 is Hyundai's smallest car. It's one of the smallest cars in the world and also one of the cheapest. The car comes with either a 1.0 or 1.2 litre engine, which is as small as it gets, making it fuel-conservative and quite easy to maintain. But it's interesting to discover that this car that weighs just 933kg is a 5-seater with ample boot space, like most saloons. It accelerates well and has a 5-speed gearbox for those with a need for speed. It comes with its fair share of external curves and also beautiful interiors, as well as a good number of modern features only found in the trendiest cars.

Simply put, the car is small but very sufficient.

But all these features and thoughtfulness fitted into such a small car was a deliberate decision by the car manufacturer to deliver not only on affordability but also on functionality. This paradigm is definitely shared by people in need of affordable housing. It is relatively easy to make a house affordable by making it small or tiny; but genius is when it is small but still thoughtfully and sufficiently houses the user.

'Sufficiency' will depend on the stage of life of the user and where s/he fits as far as her/his housing career. A studio apartment of twenty-four square meters may be sufficient for a twenty-four-year-old entry-level bachelor; but what is sufficient for him ten years later, when he is married with two opposite-sex children, may be a two- or three-bedroom apartment. And of course, since he's married, the kitchen should no longer be just a cubby-hole by the corridor, and also a pantry for storage becomes more important.

The point here is that affordable housing developers, at the design stage of development, need to think through who is their target market, and ensure that they consider how the users will interact with the space and find it sufficient, even within a tight budget. This further infers that not all affordable projects can be for all classes of people. Classifications such as student housing, starter homes, family homes, old people's homes, and the like, can be used to help streamline the users of each class of development. This breeds healthy communities based on shared commonalities and similarities regarding stage of life.

When houses are too small for the users, they may begin to act irrationally. They creatively find ways to erect attachments, re-partition space, add appendages, or even begin to squat on adjoining space or land not belonging to them. In some cases, they may transform common areas for their personal use, and it's in such cases that a beautiful project can begin to resemble a slum.

When people are space constrained, they begin to find ways to help themselves. So perhaps such actions may even be pragmatically explained as rational under the circumstances, because, as the saying goes: 'water will always find its level.'

TWENTY-FIVE

Manufacturing and Construction Must Speak

Imagine living in a world where you want to buy an item – for example, a house – and you find out that all the available houses are too expensive. But then you ask: "Can you produce a house with the specifications I want and at the price I want to pay?" And the answer you get is "Yes!" That would be a perfect world – where the manufacturing and construction industries can meet your needs.

House prices can only be as affordable as the costs of construction, and the cost of construction can only be as affordable as the building materials. These building materials are produced not by real estate agents or construction companies, but by a totally different industry – Manufacturing. Interestingly, this industry is rarely called into the room when housing affordability is being discussed. It's like there's a mental block that says manufacturing companies cannot re-engineer their products to achieve lower prices, and sometimes even better quality, to make houses cheaper.

But the loss due to this lack of communication is not affecting manufacturing as much as it's affecting construction and real estate. Take the tech industry, for instance; they have continually invested not only in creating innovative ideas but also in working with the manufacturers that fabricate the individual components that make up the technological feats. To this end, it is cheaper to produce phones, storage devices and even computers than it was many years ago. This is because tech and manufacturing speak frequently. The same can be said of the automobile, fashion and pharmaceutical industries.

In more developed countries, the construction and manufacturing industries definitely compare notes, unlike what seems to happen in developing countries. Little wonder it is more expensive to build houses in developing countries like Nigeria, Ghana and Togo than it is in countries like China or Germany. In advanced countries, the construction industry gives the manufacturing companies feedback on how their components work or are perceived by the users. This feedback is utilised to rework and produce better, faster, smaller and cheaper items and tools. This makes the construction industry more effective and efficient on a continuous basis, especially when it comes to delivering houses that are affordable.

In the production of houses, the construction industry provides the skill and labour, while manufacturing provides the materials and the tools. Both industries are equally important, and if housing is to be made affordable, the price charged by both sectors must be reconsidered to ensure affordability of the final product.

TWENTY-SIX

How Maintenance Affects Affordability

In 2015, Grammy award-winning rap star Curtis James Jackson, popularly known as 50 Cents, filed for bankruptcy a few days after losing a major legal suit requiring him to pay $5 million to his opponent. While the Connecticut bankruptcy court estimated the artist's total assets to be in the range of $10 to $50 million, he had liabilities in the same range.

Interestingly, 50 Cents had listed his 21-bedroom mansion for sale in 2007 at an offer price of $8 million, but he couldn't get a buyer, partly because the property incurred monthly maintenance costs of $67,000. This amounted to approximately $800,000 in maintenance annually – a whopping 10% of the headline sale price.

But it's not only celebrity mansions that attract high

maintenance costs; any building which is not designed from the start with the maintenance costs in mind, may be an expensive building to maintain. Maintenance costs should be of even greater priority when designing affordable housing projects.

Maintenance should be incorporated into the design and construction stages, with careful consideration as to how end users will interact with and adapt to the building. For example, in a multi-tenanted high-rise apartment block, absence of maintenance ducts and manholes will make it expensive to check or rectify plumbing, electrical and HVAC issues.

Decisions on building facades, floor heights, window locations/sizes, and floor and wall finish materials all go a long way in determining the cost of maintenance throughout the lifespan of the building. Some building materials are simply cheaper and easier to maintain than others. Also, the location and size of certain building features can inform affordability. For example, windows, if placed in an awkward location, may require the use of scaffolds or scissors lifts to clean or fix, and that is expensive. This can be avoided if, during the construction phase, consideration is given to how the building can be easily maintained during its lifespan.

There is no building that does not require some form of maintenance to keep it in good shape and function, and for some buildings this can be costly. Best practice is to annually set out a dedicated sum for property maintenance for that year. For investment properties, this is typically 5 to 25% of the annual income. If a property incurs more than this for annual maintenance, it becomes a maintenance nightmare.

It is pitiful when people can afford to buy or rent a property, but cannot afford the high maintenance charges that could easily have been avoided by a more cost-effective design or by the use of different building materials.

PART 4
// THE COMMUNITY

TWENTY-SEVEN

Affordable Housing Is Participatory not Passive

One of the most authoritative and best-referenced books in the world is the Bible. One of the many profound statements in the Bible is: "For who knows a person's thoughts except their own spirit within them?"

Think about it: no-one can fully know another person. In line with this, we can agree that the best community, neighbourhood and home that a person can live in, is the one s/he contributed to developing – because no one can know what a person wants more than the person him/herself.

In this 21st century, the best organizations understand the importance of allowing the end-user to participate in developing the products they will end up using. This is the age of tailoring, customization and personalization to suit the most individualistic customer. The most generic products, from a can of Coca Cola to an air flight experience, can now be personalised and customized. Research shows that online products that give users the flexibility of personalization are more likely to be purchased and used.

This is no different for housing or affordable housing. A residential project is less likely to experience low uptake if it has included some form of participation from customers at the planning stage, in comparison to a project that was designed and built by the development company alone.

In any community development project (a new development, urban renewal, or relocation project), there are four broad phases: planning, design, construction and maintenance. At each phase, the residents of the community can offer significant participation to the benefit of all.

One major benefit of the participatory model is that it provides affordable housing developers free market research on what customers want. This is particularly important as affordable housing developers often have budget constraints that may not allow them to afford to commission elaborate research, and yet they can't afford to take a miss at finding out what the market really wants.

Starting with the planning/conceptualization phase, a community needs assessment is best carried out via engagement tools such as interviews, questionnaires and surveys. This way, the developers can easily assess the demand for the project that is being conceptualized.

The Design stage begs for even more participation through workshops, focus groups and round table events that allow the would-be-users to express their views on not just the aesthetic concepts, but also the spatial layouts and arrangements of the project. This provides room for personalization and immediate acceptance of the project straight from the drawing board (literally).

During construction, the community maintains a significant role in comparing design with execution and also supervising the project for intent. Though probably unskilled, no one can execute this role more passionately than the would-be-users. Of course, due to health and safety considerations, physical construction site visits must be controlled and limited, but they must not be eliminated. Also, consistent project reporting will keep participants informed and able to offer suggestions.

At some point, the project is delivered, but the lifecycle does not end there. Users continue to play a participatory role in maintenance, including planning, budgeting and supervision. In addition to ensuring that quality property management is delivered, residents reserve the right to tweak service levels with maintenance officers in order to suit expectations and budget. This way, they can actively ensure that the property not only was affordable to buy, but also is affordable to live in.

TWENTY-EIGHT

Give Me a Little NIMBYism

In developed countries, NIMBYism is detested by developers and a pain in the neck for local and planning authorities. In developing and under-developed countries, NIBYism typically doesn't exist. NIMBY is actually an acronym for 'Not In My Back Yard' and it is used to label persistent residents and communities that stand against new developments or redevelopments that they believe would adversely impact their neighbourhoods, property values or businesses. NIMBYism in the UK, US, Canada and Italy has stopped the development of airports, waste management facilities, high speed rails, office blocks, and even housing projects in locations where protesters believed the development would adversely affect residents. Adverse effects can include overcrowding, pollution (air, noise, waste, etc.), environmental degradation, or even unaffordability.

In poorer countries, people may typically be too busy making ends meet to consider the impacts of private and public activities on their neighbourhoods and eventually their homes. The other day, when a friend asked me to view a property investment he was considering, I could see that the access road was just too narrow, even for a poorly planned province in Lagos, Nigeria. When I questioned why the road was irrationally the narrowest cul-de-sac ever, my friend pointed to the humongous house, built by a former politician, that seals the entire street off from the motorway.

While I was pondering how irresponsible it was not just for the politician to seal people off from standard accessibility, but also for the people to keep silent, or at least not fight hard enough to stop the injustice. I then remembered how I myself had ignored the government contractors that periodically abandoned the construction of the road right in front of my home. What's more, they would often leave heaps of rubble which sometimes prevented access to my driveway.

Some pride of place, sense of ownership, and sense of responsibility is required for sustainable, pleasurable and affordable living. Sometimes a stance needs to be taken – Not In My Back Yard!

Interestingly, a lot of NIMBYs in developed countries stand against everything this book represents – that is, they try hard to prevent affordable and social housing. Research shows that high and middle class communities usually have three major concerns about proposed affordable developments: the potential increased crime rates and reduced property values due to the intended affordable development; the imagined behaviour of the future residents; and the imagined inferior physical appearance and type of the proposed affordable homes. But if the rich and comfortable are willing to stop the poor from coming into their neighbourhoods, why are the poor never willing to fight against gentrification and schemes that make their own neighbourhoods too expensive for them to live in?

One answer to this is that as middle class neighbourhoods grow in demand and values rise, the poor initially feel it's to their benefit. But is it really? Services, amenities and other requirements for living eventually become too expensive, and the rational option is to sell and move on. And the process of moving out is even faster for renters.

But imagine a neighbourhood where existing residents do everything possible to keep property values controlled and affordable – then no one would have to move out because of rising prices. The community is not only a critical catalyst for the existence of affordable homes; even more important, it is there to ensure that homes remain affordable over time by demanding "Not In My Back Yard" when it comes to any initiative or economic movement that may inhibit affordability in the short or long term.

TWENTY-NINE

The Stakeholder Engagement Ladder

Generally speaking, when it comes to affordable housing, the first and most important factor that comes to mind is price. Many other elements such as location, size, tenure and rights come to bear, but price is the deal maker or breaker.

Milton Friedman popularized the adage "There ain't no such thing as a free lunch" – TANSTAAFL – when explaining opportunity cost and the fact that there is always a price to pay. In the affordable housing context, TANSTAAFL tells us that low prices can only be achieved by lowering what is supplied.

But if the product is stripped of features without engaging the users, it may no longer be useful. Consequently, it becomes imperative to engage end-users when seeking to remove, replace or reduce features so that the end result is acceptable.

The stakeholder engagement ladder, first designed by Sherry Arnstein in1969, can be adopted to demonstrate how social and affordable housing developers can engage would-be users at different levels, depending on the appropriateness or the level of willingness of the developer to relinquish control.

Arnstein's model holds that stakeholder engagement with the public at the lowest level can best be described as a state of Manipulation. This is because only one party – usually the government or housing development company – has full control of the decision making. This also includes when the public is engaged via surveys, questionnaires or direct feedback, but only in the sense that their feedback is just a 'rubberstamp'.

The second level of engagement is the stage of Therapy. At this level, the people are seemingly engaged, but only in a bid to change the stakeholders' views.

The third stage is Informing, which is really the first true stage of participation. At this stage, the stakeholders are notified of their rights, responsibilities and options.

The fourth stage of stakeholder engagement is Consultation. At this point, the opinions of the stakeholders are sought, and their ideas are taken into account.

The fifth level is Placation – where the stakeholders have some influence on the final decisions that are made by the housing developer; that is, the developer is willing to placate or appease them.

The sixth stage is a power-sharing scenario where the stakeholders and developers are in Partnership to deliver the housing project. Different parties have their different roles where they make the majority of the decisions.

The seventh level – Delegated Power – exists when certain management powers are delegated to the stakeholders, thereby moving stakeholders much closer to the decision making and significantly increasing participation. At this level, users and developers become co-producers of affordable housing.

The eighth and highest level is a state of Citizen Control, which has the potential to significantly produce positive results because the representatives of the stakeholders have major decision-making powers by sitting on the board or steering committee of the operating entity. This is essentially a state of self-government and derives from the premise that no one can satisfy a person better than him/herself.

Since Arnstein's 1969 model was first developed, the mode of adoption of the eight stages on the stakeholder engagement ladder – Manipulation, Therapy, Informing, Consultation, Placation, Partnership, Delegated Power and Citizen Control – has since changed from its original form. While upward movement on the stakeholder ladder was encouraged as purely positive, more recent thought holds that different stakeholders often need quite different engagement approaches to achieve optimal results.

THIRTY

How To Calculate Housing Affordability

Affordability means different things to different people. What is affordable to the Queen will not be affordable to the Queen's cleaner. In both theory and practice, the relativity of affordability makes it difficult to determine. Affordability is a moving target; it differs by location, person and circumstance. But what may be more important is to know how to measure and calculate affordability.

Academics and Housing Professionals have identified three main methods of calculating housing affordability. The first is the housing expenditure-to-income ratio. This is simply the percentage of a person's income that is spent on housing. So take, for instance, a couple who jointly earn $10,000 per annum and spend $2,000 per annum on housing; their housing expenditure-to-income is 20%. According to the housing expenditure-to-income measure, 20% is a fair figure. Mortgage providers use this measure to check if a mortgage loan is affordable for anyone seeking a mortgage. Their rule is that a household should not be spending more than 25 to 30% of their annual income on housing.

The housing expenditure-to-income measure is widely used, and 30% is widely acclaimed as the golden number beyond which unaffordability beckons. However, this measure is flawed. While a household may pay even less than 30% on housing, this does not presuppose that they will be able to meet their other basic needs, meaning they truly can't afford the home despite the measure being less than 30% of income. This added perspective leads to the second measure – the residual income approach.

The residual income approach measures housing affordability by the portion of the household income the renter can afford to pay for housing, after they have attended to their other basic needs such as feeding, transportation, basic clothing, energy, etc. This method of measure best attests to the etymology of the term: 'affordability' being the 'ability to afford.' So this way, housing affordability truly differs from person to person and place to place, dependent on the other costs the household needs to incur before leaving the remainder for housing. Consequently, some households may be able to afford to spend only 10% of their revenue on housing; while others may be able to comfortably afford to spend even 40% of their income on housing. Affordability, in this case, is dependent on their residual income.

The third measure is the incremental affordability approach, which views affordability as a concept that should be measured at different stages and not be dependent on a one-time assessment. This is especially applied to individuals or households building a home in stages or taking a piecemeal approach. Due to the time factor, the expected change in circumstances as the home development progresses, and the reduced expenditure required; the affordability level of the individual or household is not expected to remain constant.

Just in case that last paragraph was a bit confusing, don't bite your tongue just yet. Think about it in another way. Say you need to build a house for $100,000 over a 12-month period, and all you can afford at the time is 30%, which is $30,000. If you start the development with the $30,000 in your account and expend it over three months, by month four your affordability level is no longer 30%; it is now 0%. In reality, at that point, you may have saved up some additional cash; for example, $700. Consequently, what you can afford now is 10% ($700 is 10% of the $70,000 required to complete the development).

These three methods or measures are very useful, in that they provide both a standard basis and a logical theory that allows people in different parts of the world, and in different settings, to universally compute housing affordability using one of the three computation options. Though related, the three methods are extremely varied and therefore suitable for a variety of scenarios. The additional skill required by housing regulators, providers and financiers is the ability to determine which is the best and fairest measure of affordability given the circumstances. This brings us full circle to the initial conclusion that affordability means different things to different people.

THIRTY-ONE

How Culture Affects House Prices

Culture shapes the way we think. Without seeking permission, it determines the food we eat, the clothes we wear, the songs we listen to, and the places we visit. Scientists have seen that culture even "...influences the way a person's brain perceives visual stimuli such as scenes and colors" (Corey Binns).

Researchers have identified varied factors as being determinants of housing prices. These include: inflation, interest rates, per capita income, changes in population, unemployment rates, and mortgage rates. Also, some academics and economists view housing starts, legislative and taxation characteristics, increases in national income growth, land prices, construction costs, and even wages of construction workers as further determinants or elements of housing prices. But very rarely are behavioural norms and culture considered major factors in determining house prices.

In one of the most land-fertile parts of Nigeria, it is seen as taboo to sell land to non-indigenes, and so despite the fact that land in this region is arable and attractive to foreign investors and non-indigenous farmers, this taboo has posed a significant impediment to the region becoming a large-scale agriculture hub. However, some sort of parallel market now exists for land trades to daring non-indigenes – at a premium, of course.

Similarly, in India, foreigners are not legally permitted to purchase immovable property; they are only allowed to lease. If the laws of economics are anything to go by, this stifled supply can only create pent-up demand that eventually pushes prices up.

On the flip side, the Aboriginal people of mainland Australia have a cultural obligation to live in large numbers with relatives. This creates a somewhat unhealthy living environment in some areas and increases the chance of the spread of disease. The unhygienic living standards discourage interest in the buying or letting of land in these locations and as such reduce the property values.

Most studies examine macroeconomic factors as the determinants of house prices, and rightly so. But on a foundational level, the culture and norms of a people also inform property values. The UK has a liberal perspective regarding property acquisition. Foreigners can buy and trade land and buildings fairly easily. Therefore, it is no surprise that in recent years, high-net-worth Asian and Far

Eastern investors have been touted as being responsible for driving London property prices through the roof.

So while on the one hand, London's economic prosperity is responsible for international interest in its property market, her liberal and cultural openness to internationals is almost equally responsible for the demand and supply interactions that have informed the significant rise in house prices.

Cultural identity goes beyond government policy. Governments, through legislation and policing powers, may choose to permit or discourage transfer of property rights. But practical implementation is very much subject to the norms of the people. The liberality or conservativeness of a people is their prerogative, and this often differs from community to community.

THIRTY-TWO

Land sharing as a housing finance model

When Mark Twain made the oft-quoted statement "Buy land, they're not making it anymore," he was alluding to the obvious – land is finite. The total quantity of land on earth is fixed and known. According to the American Ecologist Eric Pianka, the total land surface area of the earth is about 148 million square kilometres, "of which about 33% is desert and about 24% is mountainous."

This, amongst other reasons, makes land expensive, especially in cities. Even when reclamations are done to create land, the newly created parcel derives its value from the price of the closest existing terra firma, so it is equally expensive. (That's what makes the reclamation worthwhile in the first place.)

Land acquisition marks the commencement of a housing

project, and where this expensive resource is not successfully acquired, there is no project. But where land doesn't have to be purchased as a whole, or at all, it frees up a lot of capital for the actual development of the project. This is the cloth that joint ventures are made from.

An individual or developer with sufficient capital for construction teams up with another entity that owns land (the landowner) to create a development. In this scenario, both parties collaborate to achieve their common objectives. The joint venture model may seem commonplace; however, it remains a creative way of financing housing development.

Joint ventures work well between parties that have some equity to bring to the transaction. One usually brings secured land, the other finance, and in some cases a third party throws in expertise. But when the prime land is held physically by the urban poor who are squatting in slums created at the edge of a city centre or suburb, it is impossible to enter a joint venture – because the squatters legally have nothing to bring to the table. The space they occupy is an integral part of their sustenance, so how can they give it up?

In such a scenario, a creative model that may be adopted is the concept of land sharing. In this case, de jure and de facto landowners in a community can team up to share land in order to meet their individual purposes, under one agreement. This concept was adopted and proven in Bangkok in the 1970's and 1980's. Land sharing is an arrangement where commercial developments are accommodated on lands inhabited informally or illegally by slum dwellers without utilizing powers of eviction. Under the land-sharing concept, the parties agree to share the land. On one portion, the developer erects a commercial development, while on the other portion a development is erected to re-house the slum dwellers who, up until the land-sharing-transaction, occupied the total area of the land. Land sharing replaces an eyesore slum with two good-looking developments: one for the developer and one for the erstwhile squatters.

Paul Rabe, in his 2005 paper "Land Sharing in Phnom Penh and Bangkok", holds that for a land sharing transaction to be successful, six preconditions must exist. One of these conditions is that the property market in the country where land sharing is being considered must be booming. He reasons that for land sharing to be worthwhile to private developers or government, a real estate boom must exist to put pressure on well located lands. It is this pressure that makes it economically possible for the developing party to make the concessions to redevelop a portion of the land for the urban poor. Without serious financial gains to be made on the commercial portion, it is utopic to consider that the developer will be willing to redevelop a portion for the squatters. Without a boom, eviction may not be humane, but it will be cheaper from the developer's perspective.

But it's not only a boom that is required for this concept to succeed. A well-organized and established squatter community, and a third party intermediary, are other factors that Paul Rabe considers requisite for a land-sharing agreement to be successful. In reality, the developer (private or government), who probably has the legal right to the land, needs to certify that the concessions it is willing to make will guarantee that the entire land will become accessible for its use. Should concessions be cornered by a faction of the squatters, leaving others unwilling to vacate the developer's portion, the deal will most likely collapse. The presence of an intermediary who ensures that everyone is on the same page, and that the squatters are being formed into a pseudo-formal community, will go a long way to safeguard that even a handshake deal will translate to all parties having their fair access to land.

PART 5
// THE INDIVIDUAL

THIRTY-THREE

You Need A "Housing Career"

One reason we have professional careers is to provide for our needs, the basic three being food, clothing and housing. But the phrase "housing career" does not suggest you should be a career housing practitioner just because housing is so important, but rather that the housing solution for every individual should be progressively dynamic, that is, having a life cycle – like a good professional career.

It is important that citizens have a housing career because housing is a capital good that requires a lot of time and financial resources even to produce a single unit. Hence, for housing supply to be sustainable, the demand must equally be sustainable. It would take a significantly longer time for the housing deficit of any country to be met if the demand kept increasing irresponsibly or irrationally.

A typical professional career starts at entry level; low paying, plain vanilla, and with little or no experience required. As the worker progresses, s/he moves into middle management, becomes more of a specialist, and handles more complex and larger responsibilities, all of which naturally warrants higher remuneration. With the exception of family businesses and start-ups, it would be an anomaly to expect certain magnitudes of responsibility too early in one's career. In general, job responsibilities and remunerations tend to increase over time in line with social and demographic stratifications.

The housing demands of the average urban dweller should follow similar patterns. Space and tenure requirements should increase to match the social and demographic stratifications of individuals; otherwise the result could be unsustainable demand. Young school leavers would typically rent a small starter home, get married and have a bigger flat (2 to 3 bedrooms), and then transit into a family home (3 to 4 bedrooms) if they have children. At this stage, they should also be considering a more permanent tenure (ownership) as against renting for mobility when they started out.

Should every university graduate expect to own his or her own "pad," and every newlywed move into their own family home straight from the altar, this would set unrealistic expectations that would not be met even in first world countries. Of course, there are exceptions to every rule, and some families, and even sovereign states, can afford to offer young graduates apartments upon graduating, or lavish new couples with 4-bedroom houses as wedding gifts, but such practice is not the norm.

In approaching housing affordability and accessibility, it's important to help people in need of housing to understand that they should have a housing career. It's important that they understand that housing is both a process and a lifecycle. No individual will have the same type of housing need all through his/her life. Early in one's career, mobility and a low upfront cost are very important, and renting small apartments offers this. Later in one's career, stability and space become more paramount, and this is when home ownership is the major consideration. At this stage in life, it is typically expected that the earning potential of the individual or family has greatly increased due to the fact that the earning individuals have more experience and skill. Also, it is expected that by this time, the individual/couple has saved up enough to access a mortgage or make an outright purchase.

As such, a good number of people do not have to fret too much about housing; they just need to ensure they are at the right stage of their housing career.

THIRTY-FOUR

The Race for Space

Starting in the mid-1950's, two world super-powers – the Soviet Union and the United States – began a rivalry to demonstrate supremacy in space and lunar travel, each country striving hard and fast to land the first human in space and on the moon. This contention, which would end in the late 1990's, was dubbed the "Space Race."

The Soviet Union won the first battle, in October 1957, when the Russian astronaut Yuri Gagarin became the first man in space; but the U.S would be the first to land humans on the moon, in the summer of 1969 with the Apollo 11 team.

Many have rightly argued how risky, expensive and

distracting the space race was; and it wasn't until after the end of the unnecessary enmity, and the agreement between Russia and the U.S. to cooperate regarding space operations, that the biggest research strides were made.

Today, a different kind of race exists. It's a race for space, rather than a race to space – a race to acquire and hold land and property. Today, there is a global land rush, which is resulting not only in unaffordable housing but also in food volatility. As less land remains available for farming, food shortages are reflected by hikes in prices.

Individuals and organizations all over the world have a strong desire to be first, to gain territory and to demonstrate supremacy, just as in the space race. So what is now prevalent is a corrupt and inequitable distribution of land, where the political and upper classes benefit to the detriment of the general population – and this creates land scarcity and an unaffordable housing situation.

Land grabbing is wiping out communities, eroding the livelihood of families, and disenfranchising individuals via conquest, corruption and commerce. Even when land is bought commercially from its previous owners who sold it because they were too poor to keep it, the sale does little to enrich the original owner; rather it impoverishes them even more because they then don't have a home.

Not all possessions should be sold to the highest bidder, offered to the first comer, or given to the strongest contender. If all things were distributed in such a manner, people would easily trade or buy other people's wives and children. No matter how broke a nation is, it will not sell all its land to the highest bidder; if it did, it would cease to exist. Laissez faire cannot be the order in such circumstances. Individuals and organisations engaging in large land and property acquisitions should ensure such transactions do not further impoverish small subsistence farmers and less-privileged families if they are irrationally selling their only home or their source of livelihood. Anti-trust laws may not exist or be applicable to forestall hostile land transactions, but participating individuals owe it to society to curb its own race for space.

Irrational and excessive demand for housing reduces the incentive for developers and housing suppliers to be creative and strive for higher quality. When a supplier has too much demand, s/he doesn't have to try hard to please his/her clients.

THIRTY-FIVE

Five Myths Of Rental Housing

Should a dinner conversation with friends ever drift toward who owns or rents the home they live in, those who rent will immediately be mentally classified by all (including the renters themselves) as being plagued by some or all of the following myths:

Renting is for the poor; the rich own their homes
This is the first and greatest myth of rental housing. It's important to note that housing is the basic human need, not home ownership. It doesn't matter if you're renting, co-habiting or owner-occupying, what is essential is that you are housed. Renting affords mobility, flexibility and cash flow management, which may be the objectives of even the super-rich. Renting allows people to live in different parts of a country or the world, at different times, without being fixed to a particular house. Renting gives users the choice to live in locations or house types one may not be able to afford

to own but can afford to lease.

Everyone owns in rich countries
This is a myth and it couldn't be farther from the truth. 60% of Germans live in rented accommodation, 34% in the USA, and 31% in the UK. In Niger Republic, on the other hand, 7% rent, and in India, 11% rent. In most cities, more people rent than own: 55% of New Yorkers rent; 41% of Londoners rent; and a whopping 89% rent in Berlin (Source: UN Habitat). Renting is not bad; it's often just the reasonable decision to make. In the most populous cities, migrants make up the bulk of the labour force and indeed of the entire population. These people are merely transiting, albeit this may be for long periods, like 10 years. What's clear is that the city they choose to live in is primarily determined by their jobs. And in this case it is typically a wise decision to rent rather than take on a mortgage or expend all one's savings to own a home in a town they may no longer live in because they have to change their job or their locality.

Home ownership offers people a better life and also savings on annual housing costs
This is an outright lie and is partly responsible for a series of bankruptcies, forced sales and derelict houses defacing the environment. When people believe this lie – that home ownership will give them a better life and enable them save on annual housing – they are deceived into buying homes that they may be able to afford to buy but can't afford to keep. Like most other goods that can be bought, there is always the cost of maintenance. Annual maintenance costs of houses can be as low as 2% of the capital value, but can

also be as high as 20%. This figure is never zero, as there is always a cost for maintenance – which some homeowners may choose to ignore, but it will eventually bite them and may leave their homes derelict and their lives worse off than before.

Everyone wishes to be a homeowner

This is sometimes an incorrect assumption. In some countries of the world, it is typically much less stressful and much cheaper to rent a home than to own one. Homeowners need to comply with a myriad of environmental, tax, planning, fire/safety, utility, insurance and even political regulations to keep their home. Renters, on the other hand, have fewer requirements to fulfil. This may be hard for some people to digest, but if time, freedom and flexibility are more important to you than the bragging rights of homeownership, you may prefer to rent..

Rental housing is not well maintained

This final myth is not unfounded, as there are certainly bad landlords. However, good landlords are not necessarily good, but they are wise. Maintaining one's investment in rental property is really just ensuring that the property continues to have uptake and at a good rate. It also ensures that the property remains in a good structural and physical state so that it continues to be a good source of income. Often times, maintenance costs can easily be recouped through rent increments or the simple fact that you have good paying tenants and never have voids.

So as you read through the myths I have described, you may

have disagreed with some of them. Certainly, not all myths are applicable to all geographic locations; they are heavily influenced by social demographics and culture. Overall, there are five broad classifications of housing tenure: ownership, renting, co-housing, squatting and homelessness. Clearly, renting is not the worst of these.

THIRTY-SIX

Housing as a Process

There is a large expanse of land.

But before it can be occupied, it must be fitted with roads, drains, sidewalks, power and water. It must also be sub-divided into plots with zoning that determines what may be built and how it should be built. Then, when a would-be homeowner manages to get a plot, s/he must still ensure the building is built in line with the building codes and must get a certification for occupation, post-construction, before it can be inhabited.

It almost seems as if the existence of building standards serves to prohibit housing. It's so much easier to buy a house from a developer, housing association or the government than to take a stab at building a house oneself. But that's usually more expensive. The situation is even worse in developed countries, such as the US or Canada, that have much more regulated real estate and construction markets.

The biggest objection to allowing for more flexibility, which would encourage incremental self-construction of homes, is that it would lead to lowered standards – a position that is up for debate.

> *"When dwellers control the major decisions and are free to make their own contributions in the design, construction or management of their housing, both this process and the environment produced stimulate individual and social well being. When people have no control over, nor responsibility for, key decisions in the housing process, on the other hand, dwelling environments may instead become a barrier to personal fulfillment and a burden on the economy."*

– *John Turner (1972)*

It was also Turner who first brought forward the idea of housing as a process – in his book Freedom to Build. He holds that authorities and decision makers need to move past seeing housing as just a noun and see it as a verb – an action word. Housing as a noun is essentially seeing it as a commodity that provides shelter; but in its verb form, it is the process of providing shelter or accommodation.

Under this "housing as a process" paradigm, success is no longer achieved when a safe and dry house is erected according to specifications; rather, it is measured by the ease of building one's home. This may be self-built or built by a contractor; incremental or turnkey. This flexibility allows for more options and opportunities for housing to be on the individual's terms.

Quality of materials, functionality of design, compliance with building codes and zoning laws, building characteristics, and particular features are all important, but they focus only on the final product – the house. The housing process precedes and supersedes this. Housing starts with a need and a desire by individuals and by households. As such, they cannot be passive beneficiaries receiving homes as hand-downs from government agencies, housing associations or even private developers.

Home users must be the principal actors in their home delivery process.

THIRTY-SEVEN

No Title But Entitled

The sovereignty of every country is determined by the existence and enforcement of its laws. Laws are important for guiding the behaviour of visitors, residents, citizens, and the governments of a nation. Where the law is suspended in a country, it is said to be in a state of emergency.

The United Nations was established in 1945 and currently has 193 member states, which include all the G8 countries – Canada, France, Germany, Italy, Japan, Russia, the United Kingdom, and the United States. The member states also include developing countries, such as India, Indonesia, Eritrea, Ghana and Nigeria. All member countries are bound by the articles of the United Nations charter.

As far back as 1948, the Universal Declaration of Human Rights, which was adopted by the United Nations General Assembly, identified adequate housing as an integral part of the fundamental human right to an adequate standard of living. This international law has been recognized and referenced by other laws, treaties and agreements globally and within specific jurisdictions.

Not wanting this law to be subjected to narrow interpretation, the United Nations Committee on Economic, Social and Cultural Rights further elucidated the extent to which this law should be applied globally. According to the committee, the right to adequate housing includes freedoms: freedom from forced evictions, freedom from arbitrary interference in one's home, and freedom to choose one's residence.

Secondly, the committee held that the law expressly infers that adequate housing must provide more than four walls and a roof. For shelter to qualify as housing, it must have a secure tenure as well as the provision of facilities and infrastructure; and it must be affordable, habitable, accessible, culturally adequate, and reasonably located. This is the law and all member states are bound by it.

Also, a number of countries have gone ahead and included the right to adequate housing in their constitutions. For example, Article 4 of the Constitution of Mexico (1983) states: "Every family has the right to enjoy decent and proper housing. The law shall establish the instruments and necessary supports to reach the said goal."

Article 65 of the Constitution of Portugal (1976) states: "All have the right, both personally and for their family, to a dwelling of adequate size that meets satisfactory standards of hygiene and comfort and preserves personal and family privacy."

In India, adequate housing is provided for in Article 21 of the Indian Constitution (1949) in the "Right to Life" section.

Article 26 of the Constitution of South Africa (1996) states: "Everyone has the right to have access to adequate housing. The State must take reasonable legislative and other measures, within its available resources, to achieve the progressive realization of this right. No one may be evicted from their home, or have their home demolished, without an order of court made after considering all the relevant circumstances. No legislation may permit arbitrary evictions."

In spite of these laws and the commitment of UN member states to uphold the tenets of the commission, it is estimated that 1.6 billion people in the world lack adequate housing (Habitat, 2015). For example, in Nigeria, there are 24.4 million homeless people (UNHCR, 2007); 51% of Ghana's urban residents live in slums (Cities Alliance, 2013); and 7.5 million South Africans lack adequate housing (IRIN News, 2007).

The laws are available, globally and in some cases nationally, but what is missing in most jurisdictions is implementation and enforcement. These laws just seem to be suspended, despite the fact that a state of emergency has not been declared. Even refugees and internally displaced persons "have a right to be restored to them any housing, land or property of which they were arbitrarily and unlawfully deprived," according to principle 2 of the Pinheiro Principles. That people don't have title to land or property does not mean they are not entitled to it. Every human being has the right to adequate housing.

Note: The UN Habitat Factsheet 21 (Revision 1) – The right to adequate housing (2009) was a major resource for writing this piece.

THIRTY-EIGHT

The Mystery of Capital

In 2013, the Nigerian economy was recalculated, and suddenly it "became" the largest economy in Africa, beating the erstwhile top African economy – South Africa. But the Nigerian economy did not abruptly grow larger overnight due only to the re-computation of the nation's GDP using revised prices. New sectors, which were previously not counted in Nigeria's GDP computations (left out because they were considered the 'informal' economy) were added. The new additions included e-commerce, telecommunications and entertainment. This means Nollywood – the third largest movie industry in the world – was until 2013 categorised as part of the informal economy in Nigeria.

This is the mystery of capital; the capital existed but was not captured, so it did not count, and Nigeria's economy was seen as much smaller than it actually was. In reality, a nation's gross domestic product is what it is; records don't produce or reduce GDP in actual terms. But the records are what give the nation its valuation, and if something is not counted, it does not count. Public information and records are much more linked to wealth than one would think. Unfortunately, this is the curse of developing and underdeveloped countries; information and records are seen as some sort of luxury or voluntary add-on.

Most land and houses in both urban and rural parts of West African countries lack proper title, and as such they fail to count as capital for their owners. This was the same in Peru until the economist Hernando De Soto went on a crusade to combat this in his home country. In his best seller, The Mystery of Capital, he articulated how the lack of proper land titles prevents property owners from utilizing this asset to secure finances for enterprise and living.

Little wonder that property with a registered title is more valuable than an identical property without title. Property titles authenticate ownership and give credence for exchange and for increase in value. Otherwise, it would be dead capital, at best.

The cheapest houses tend to have poor or no title. But houses without good title cannot be purchased with a mortgage or a secured loan. The same goes for land without proper title; it can't be used to secure a construction loan for the development of the land. As such, improper titling limits the affordability of a land owner, even after he has acquired the land – which ought to serve as security to release further capital through a loan or investment. Similarly, when a capital good cannot be purchased in whole or in part by a loan, it becomes much more unaffordable. This is the mystery of capital.

Succinctly, the mystery of capital shows that capital is not fully created by just owning an asset; capital is created by having statutory or widely accepted evidence of ownership of the asset. This further demonstrates that the availability or non-availability of capital is a primary factor that informs housing affordability.

THIRTY-NINE

Mind the Gap

The global housing gap is enormous. According to the McKinsey Global Institute, 235 million urban households currently live in substandard housing, while 106 million additional low-income households are projected to face the affordable housing challenge by 2025. This will affect 1.6 billion people, which represents one-third of the world's urban population!

This shows a growing demand for affordable housing, and interestingly it is not just by the poor. The gap between housing supply and demand is the result of a blended cocktail of financial constraints, construction sector inefficiencies, poor policies, land supply blockages and a lack of political will.

World population is growing; the world urban population stood at 54% in 2015, overtaking rural population for the first time ever, and is predicted to grow to 66% by 2050. By then, seven countries are projected to account for 50% of the world's population: United States, Nigeria, China, India, Pakistan, Indonesia and DR Congo (RICS).

Developing and underdeveloped countries urgently need to mind the gap.

Households are getting financially overstretched more than ever, and if housing needs are not checked and met, more people will be homeless than previously. But the primary responsibility to "mind this gap" does not rest with governments, professionals, the community or the private sector; it rests with the individual.

Each individual is a product of past and present choices. While fate deals heavy blows, the individual reserves the right to stand tall or to lie down defeated. Four features are required to be adequately housed: the home must be appropriately located; the tenure must be secure; the housing quality must be adequate; and the house must have sufficient services. The choice to ensure that these are met within the household budget and earning potential is a personal one.

It's just as irresponsible for a person to squander resources on frivolities as it is for a government not to make provisions within the fiscal budget for housing delivery. Also, citizens cannot point accusing fingers at developers seeking to maximise profits when they have not maximised their own financial capabilities to meet their own housing needs.

While everyone has the right to adequate housing, that right equally confers responsibility: the responsibility to live within ones means; the responsibility to have and follow a housing career; the responsibility to budget and pay house rents when due; the responsibility to carry out the necessary due diligence before buying or renting property.

Primarily, the individual holds the responsibility to determine if a home is affordable or not, and the responsibility to mind the gap between the housing you may demand and the housing you really need.

FORTY

Why people reject some affordable housing projects

In their book Principles of Marketing, Kotler and his co-authors explain that products are like cabbage, having multi-layers. The innermost layer is the core feature, representing the most basic reason why the product is bought. As you progress outward, several augmented features layer this core. Augmented features, no matter how attractive they are to the buyer, are not the fundamental reason the product is bought in the first place, but interestingly they often determine which particular product is purchased or not.

In the hierarchy of human needs, housing ranks second – after food. Yet, like every other product, housing has both core and augmented features. The core feature of a house is to provide shelter, but as important as that is, no one chooses to buy a particular house just for that reason. The augmented features may include location, design, size, construction quality, etc., and these features influence people to choose a particular house over other available alternatives.

Similarly, every particular house has different classes of attributes. These are dwelling attributes, neighbourhood attributes, and abstract attributes. Clearly understanding these attributes helps providers and other stakeholders properly dimension the multifaceted concept of housing.

Dwelling attributes include the floor area (actual size), number of rooms, number of bathrooms, quality of construction (or type of finishes and materials), design (layout), built-in features (e.g. air conditioning, heating), plot size, age of the dwelling, etc.

Neighbourhood attributes refer to access to local public services (e.g. public transport) and other neighbourhood amenities such as recreational facilities and proximity to work, schools health care centres and shopping.

Abstract attributes may include the contract conditions, land tenure, property title, and existing property rights such as restrictive covenants, easements and the like. These features are described as abstract because they are intangible, vague and may even seem ambiguous. But abstract features are very important in that, though property is a physical asset, it is the abstract interest in property that is exchanged through a sale or lease. Property title, for instance, is the single most important factor to consider in purchasing a property.

In delivering sustainable affordable housing, providers must seek to attain the right mix of housing attributes and not just focus on low cost. Focusing on cost alone would amount to a myopic view on just the core and forgetting about the augmented features. As much as low and middle-income earners may require affordable housing, they should not embrace a scheme purely based on price.

Logical as it seems, that last statement may not hold true in developing countries where the housing shortages are chronic. People will accept affordable houses based purely on low price, even though the augmented features are far removed from what is required. However, in these circumstances the buyer will not have been sustainably housed – because as the joys of low price wear off, the realities of their true requirements set in, creating a new problem called 'under-housing'.

FORTY-ONE

And Still I See No Changes

A "nd still I see no changes" was the opening line of a hit song by Tupac Amaru Shakur, one of the all time great American rap artists. The song Changes was the artist's 1998 posthumous memoir that spoke to the changes needed in America at the time, especially from the point of view of a coloured or black American.

In the second stanza of the song, Tupac emphatically states that America is not ready to see a black president – and indeed didn't have one until eleven years later. All through the song, he speaks of seemingly insurmountable challenges facing coloured people and preventing them from getting ahead in life.

Oftentimes, life's challenges seem too big to be defeated. Likewise, affordable housing sometimes seems too utopic to become reality. The magnitude and multi-dimensional nature of the actions needed to bring about a solution can lead one to believe that it is impossible. But like Tupac's comment about the possibility of a black American presidency, we sometimes do see changes more quickly than we had expected.

In 1919, the UK saw significant changes when Sir Lloyd George, then Prime Minister, started the "Homes Fit for Heroes" campaign that saw the emergence of council flats that affordably housed British citizens for well over seven decades, and in some cases still do. In 1980, the UK once again saw changes when under Margaret Thatcher, the "Right to Buy" scheme enabled over six million people to buy the council apartments they lived in at very generous prices.

Having lived primarily in a developing country, but also visiting first world countries, I know that it is so easy to be filled with dissatisfaction, complaints and regrets for one's home country. Everything just seems much better organised and much more advanced in Europe and America. Even Dubai and Singapore that started their developmental agendas relatively recently are now super-shiny and seem to have achieved first-world status. So as we return from a foreign trip, we feel like blurting out, like Tupac: "And still I see no changes!"

But that's not totally true. There have been both small and large changes. Air travel, telecommunications, internet penetration, financial systems, entertainment, average education levels, health and hygiene – to mention just a few – have changed and improved over the years in countries like Nigeria and Ghana. Outside of war, terrorism and internal displacement, most developing countries have seen some significant improvements. These changes may not be as visible or as impactful as we desire, but it's important to recognise them and celebrate them – and to be an advocate for continued change.

The responsibility to see the possibilities for change starts with the individual. The individual needs to make an active decision to think about how to change and transform various aspects of society.

Affordable housing starts is an example of how we can begin to enact the changes that we desire, and that will benefit large numbers of individuals.

// CONCLUSION

FORTY-TWO

A House Has Five Sides

The proverbial house has five sides – four walls and a roof. At lunch or dinner, you can decide not to have a side or two for that meal, but you can't afford to live in a house that is missing one of the sides. Likewise, when it comes to adequate and affordable housing, all sides are critical.

As noted, the five sides are: the Government, the Private Sector, Professionals, the Community, and the Individual. It is impractical to achieve affordable housing without all five parties. Attempts can be made to achieve affordable housing even when one or two parties are yet to get on board, but like a house with no roof or a missing side wall, it will not be able to survive all the seasons unless the missing parties join the effort.

A five-sided house being likened to affordable housing is a natural analogy. Like each side of a house, the role each party plays in housing delivery is both distinct and critical. The private sector can never play the role of the government, and the individual cannot assume the role of the community. Professionals play their part and it would be perilous for their part to be played by non-professionals.

Indeed, the idiom popularized by Abraham Lincoln has become very apt: "A house divided against itself cannot stand." For an affordable house to stand and keep standing, more than one party is required. To start with, the concept of affordability is marked by ambiguity and is an alien in private-sector circles. The Private Sector is wired to sell a product at a mark-up compared to its cost of construction. Professionals, the Community, and even Individuals all hold this same position. The contrary worldview – that homes can and should be delivered at lower than cost – is held uniquely by Government. Only Government can afford to lead the charge to subsidize housing, and in more ways than one. This is usually the starting point in the affordable housing journey, akin to the foundation of a house.

The Private Sector must rethink housing delivery and take on the additional pressure to ensure it is delivered at less than market prices, that is, make it affordable by using sustainable finance, construction and management techniques. Furthermore, they must be selective in deciding who accesses the affordable housing – to ensure it is not simply transferred to speculators who immediately or eventually resell at open market prices.

The Professionals are the brains that whip up the thoughts of housing promoters. They must be able to interpret and build the homes affordably – otherwise the process is truncated. Even when housing is built, the Professionals must ensure it is managed and maintained affordably, so that individuals and households not only can afford to buy or rent the homes, but also can afford to live in them.

To keep an affordable house standing, the Community plays an irreplaceable role. The voice of the community must be heard to ensure housing promoters build homes affordably and keep them maintained at an affordable price. They must also work together to ensure their neighbourhoods are not gentrified, which means they would no longer be able to afford to live in their homes.

At the crux of the issue is the role of the Individual. The individual is the highest decision-making body when it comes to determining the affordability of housing! S/he must decide to take responsibility for his/her housing career and stay the course.

Individuals in developed nations have done this fairly well and consistently for many years, and as a result they have developed sustainable affordable and social housing sectors. In such nations, housing is a major issue not only in bars or nursing homes, but in election cycles, in family expenditure budgeting, and in tax filings.

Individuals in developing and underdeveloped countries must take responsibility for their housing career and stay the course. They must rise and continue to rise in their demand for affordable homes from all other parties that must equally play crucial roles. As the Rwandan Proverb goes: "If you are building a house and a nail breaks, do you stop building or do you change the nail?"

// NOTES

Chapter 1
Reregulation and Residualization in Dutch social Housing: a critical Evaluation of new Policies by Joris Hoekstra (PhD) Research for the Built Environment, TU Delf

Assessing the social and economic impact of affordable housing investment A report prepared for the G15 and National Housing Federation by Frontier Economics September 2014

Dutch social housing in a nutshell by Aedes – Dutch Association of Social Housing Organizations July 2013

Class Notes on Introduction to (Social) Housing in Netherlands by Ellen Guerts for the 2016 Developing Social Housing Projects Course, Institute of Housing and Urban Development, Erasmus University

Class Notes on Social Housing policy trends by Julia Skinner for the 2016 Developing Social Housing Projects Course, Institute of Housing and Urban Development, Erasmus University

Class Notes on Social Housing Policies and Tenure Trends by Ellen Geurts for the 2016 Developing Social Housing Projects Course, Institute of Housing and Urban Development, Erasmus University

Chapter 2
Wakely, P. (2014). Urban Public Housing strategies in developing countries: whence and whither paradigms, policies, programmes

Class Notes on Social Housing Policies and Tenure Trends by

Ellen Geurts for the 2016 Developing Social Housing Projects Course, Institute of Housing and Urban Development, Erasmus University

UN-Habitat (2006), Enabling Shelter Strategies: Review of Experience from two decades of implementation,Nairobi, UN-Habitat

Chapter 3
Class Notes on Social Housing Policies and Tenure Trends by Ellen Geurts for the 2016 Developing Social Housing Projects Course, Institute of Housing and Urban Development, Erasmus University

UN-Habitat (2006), Enabling Shelter Strategies: Review of Experience from two decades of implementation,Nairobi, UN-Habitat

The State of Housing in the EU 2015 - A Housing Europe Review by Housing Europe, the European Federation for Public Cooperative and Social Housing 2015

Quotations on the Jefferson memorial culled from www.monticello.org

Chapter 4
A complete guide to the low-income housing tax credit program by Neal Hefferren 13th June 2017 culled from www.propertymetrics.com

The low-income housing tax credit program culled from www.wespath.com
National Library Board of Singapore resources

The Economist – Why 80% of Singaporeans live in government built flats

Chapter 7
Housing finance across countries: New data and analysis by Anton Badev, Thorsten Beck, Ligia Vado, and Simon Walley – for The World Bank January 2014

Reform of the mortgage interest tax relief system, policy uncertainty and precautionary savings in the Netherlands by Mauro Mastrogiacomo (De Nederlandsche Bank, VU University Amsterdam, Netspar)

Chapter 8
Hills, John (2001) Inclusion or exclusion? The role of housing subsidies and benefits. Urban studies, 38 (11). pp. 1887-1902

Assessing the Economic Benefits of Public Housing by Econsult Corporation January 2007

Gladwell, Malcolm. What the Dog Saw: And Other Adventures. New York: Little, Brown and Co., 2009.

Is It Possible to Measure the Value of Social Housing? Michael Buzzelli, CPRN Research Report September 2009

Chapter 9
A blueprint for addressing the global affordable housing

challenge by the McKinsey Global Institute October 2014

Chapter 10
A blueprint for addressing the global affordable housing challenge by the McKinsey Global Institute October 2014

www.toki.gov.tr

Chapter 11
Successes and Failures of PPP Projects presentation by Vickram Cuttaree 17 June, 2008

http://gpf.org.za/projects-funded/pennyville

Class Notes on PPPs in Social Housing by Carely Pennink for the 2016 Developing Social Housing Projects Course, Institute of Housing and Urban Development, Erasmus University

Chapter 12
Dutch social housing in a nutshell by Aedes – Dutch Association of Social Housing Organizations July 2013

Journal Oeconomique 1751, Article by the French minister of finance.

Chapter 13
A blueprint for addressing the global affordable housing challenge by the McKinsey Global Institute October 2014

2016 Global Accounts of private registered providers by UK Homes & Communities Agency, February 2017

IPD Netherlands Annual Social Housing Index by MSCI

IPD Netherlands Annual Social Property Index by MSCI

Chapter 14
www.archdaily.com/10775/quinta-monroy-elemental

Chapter 15
Third-Party Affordability Monitoring Handbook for Mass Housing 40B Homeownership Projects

Chapter 16
www.national-lottery.co.uk/life-changing/where-the-money-goes

Chapter 18
20 Years of Enabling Shelter Strategy: The role of housing in sustainable urbanisation by Claudio Acioly Jr., presentation at the 52nd IFHP Congress, 2008

The Right to Adequate Housing, Fact Sheet 21 Rev. 1 by UN Habitat

Chapter 19
The Registry. (2014, December 11). Mercy Housing Com-

pletes 1180 Fourth Street Affordable Housing Designed by Mithun|Solomon and Kennerly Architecture in San Francisco [Blog post]

www.acor.com.au/lilyfield-housing-redevelopment-nsw

www.affordablehousingonline.com/housing-search/California/Los-Angeles/Casa-

www.calgrom3.com/index.php/pennyville

www.gpf.org.za/Projects-Funded/pennyville

www.urbamonde.org/#/en/community/304

Chapter 20

Bringing central Johannesburg back to life By Tim Smart - www.bbc.com/news/business-35830583

Johnathan Leibman TedX Talk at Stellenboch - www.youtube.com/watch?v=QjRvqwMOx-Q

Chapter 22

www.retrlettire.com/projects/the-tapestry/

www.pocketliving.com/projects/development/21

www.kevindalyarchitects.com/projects/#/project/broadway-housing

Chapter 23
The Language of Houses by Alison Lurie, Haper Collins
www.washingtonpost.com/entertainment/books/alison-
luries-the-language-of-houses
www.lilac.coop

www.dbarchitect.com/project_detail/146/Bayview

www.artefacts.co.za

Chapter 24
www.cardekho.com/carmodels/Hyundai/Hyundai_i10

Chapter 26
www.realtor.com/news/celebrity-real-estate/rapper-50-
cent-mansion-wont-sell/

Chapter 27
1 Corinthians 2:11, The Bible, New International Version,
Zondervan

Class Notes on Community Participation by Julia Skinner for
the 2016 Developing Social Housing Projects Course, Institute
of Housing and Urban Development, Erasmus University

Chapter 28
Why Are There NIMBYs? By William A. Fischel

Chapter 29

Class Notes on Involving the Community and other Stakeholders when Designing Social Housing Environments by Liesl Vivier for the 2016 Developing Social Housing Projects Course, Institute of Housing and Urban Development, Erasmus University

Class Notes on Community Participation by Julia Skinner for the 2016 Developing Social Housing Projects Course, Institute of Housing and Urban Development, Erasmus University

Chapter 30

Affordable Housing in the Global South Edited by jan Bredenoord, Paul van Lindert and Peer Smets, Routledge 2014

Chapter 31

www.scientificamerican.com/article/the-hidden-power-of-culture/

Chapter 32

Land Sharing in Phnom Penh and Bangkok by Paul Rabe, 2005

Class Notes on Provision of Land for Social Housing by Paul Rabe for the 2016 Developing Social Housing Projects Course, Institute of Housing and Urban Development, Erasmus University

Chapter 33

Intentions to move from homelessness to social inclusion: the role of participation beliefs, attitudes and prior behaviour by Christian, J et al , 2016

The housing pathways of young people in the UK by David Clapham, 2017

21st Century housing careers and Australia's housing future: Literature Review by Andrew Beer et al, 2006

Chapter 35
Class Notes on Social Housing Policies and Tenure Trends by Ellen Geurts for the 2016 Developing Social Housing Projects Course, Institute of Housing and Urban Development, Erasmus University

Chapter 36
Turner, J., (1972), Housing as a verb, in: Turner,J., FichterR., (Eds.), Freedom to Build: Dweller control of the housing process. The Macmillan Company.

Chapter 37
The UN Habitat Factsheet 21 (Revision 1) – The right to adequate housing, 2009

Class Notes on Provision of Land for Social Housing by Paul Rabe for the 2016 Developing Social Housing Projects Course, Institute of Housing and Urban Development, Erasmus University

Chapter 38
The Mystery of Capital by Hernando De Soto, 2000. Black Swan.

Chapter 39
A blueprint for addressing the global affordable housing challenge by the McKinsey Global Institute, October 2014

Our changing world: let's be ready by RICS, 2015.

Chapter 40
Principles of Marketing by Philip Kotler et al, 2008. Financial Times / Prentice Hall.

Class Notes on Social Housing policy trends by Julia Skinner for the 2016 Developing Social Housing Projects Course, Institute of Housing and Urban Development, Erasmus University

Chapter 41
Changes by Tupac Shakur, 1998. Interscope / Desthrow Records.

www.historic-uk.com/HistoryUK/HistoryofBritain/Lloyd-George

www.theguardian.com/society/2015/aug/26/right-to-buy-margaret-thatcher-david-cameron-housing-crisis

CPSIA information can be obtained
at www.ICGtesting.com
Printed in the USA
LVHW030409180322
713694LV00005B/1040